THE MAGIC OF IRELAND
H.V. MORTON

THE MAGIC OF IRELAND
H. V. MORTON

EYRE METHUEN LONDON

Publisher's Foreword

H. V. Morton's first travel books came out almost half a century ago. As a young reporter he drove his bullnosed Morris to the farthest corners of Britain and Ireland, following no special plan but returning with material for his 'In Search' series. These famous books, starting with *In Search of England* in 1927, have been read and reread by millions of enthusiasts. They appeal to readers of any age, who often retrace Morton's own journeys and write to tell him so.

The reason for this is simple. Travel writing at its best calls for imagination as much as for the writing skill to observe and report. Morton has imagination of two kinds. He can project himself back into history and capture distant events and the actors on stage at a particular place he visits. And when the people he meets are contemporaries, of the twentieth century, he understands them and their work with a sympathy they repay. This is just what we would like to manage on our own travels.

This volume presents selections from H. V. Morton's *In Search of Ireland*, together with 160 pages of photographs in colour and mono-chrome which both complement and add to Morton's text.

First published in 1978
by Eyre Methuen Ltd
11 New Fetter Lane, London EC4P 4EE

Based on extracts taken from
In Search of Ireland (Methuen 1930)

Copyright © 1930 and 1978 H. V. Morton

Edited by Patricia Haward

Filmset by Keyspools Ltd, Golborne, Lancs
Printed and bound in Great Britain by
Hazell Watson & Viney Ltd
Aylesbury, Bucks

ISBN 0 413 31290 9

CONTENTS

Publisher's Foreword 4

**1
Dublin** 7

**2
Wicklow to Cork** 39

**3
Kerry** 77

**4
Limerick to Connemara** 101

**5
Croagh Patrick to Tara** 133

Acknowledgements 160

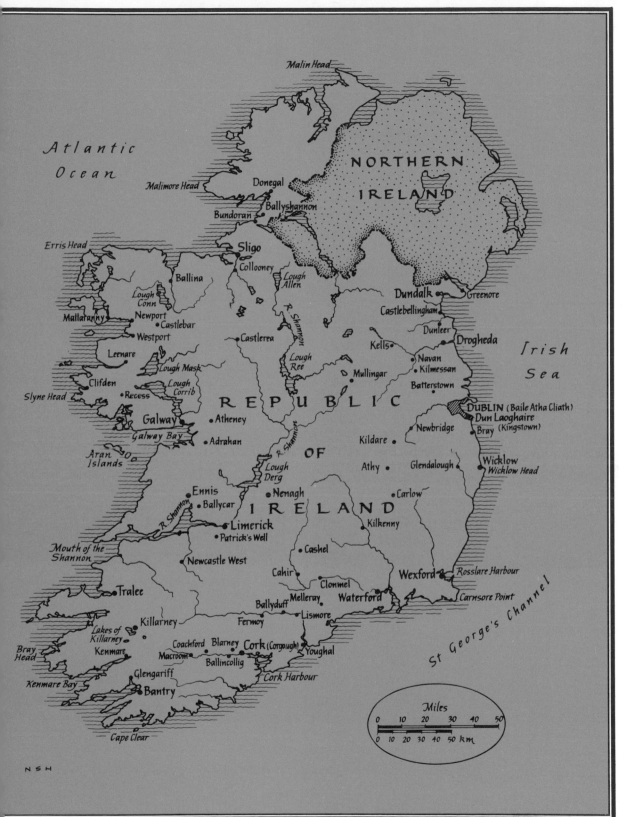

1
DUBLIN

The roses on the saloon tables trembled slightly and shed an occasional petal into the salad. That, and a furtive creak of mahogany, was the only indication that we were at sea. If we glanced through the portholes we saw that the Holyhead boat moved towards Ireland over calm, green waters. It was June.

There were three American families on board, on their way, I suppose, to visit in a Daimler car the village which their ancestors left on foot. There were Englishmen with rods and golf clubs, our usual missionaries of leisure, hearty, pink Englishmen, washed and polished; and there were Englishwomen of the country kind in tweed costumes who always remind me of a phrase employed exclusively by publishers – 'these companionable volumes'.

Two priests walked the deck. They were as foreign as Frenchmen on a Channel boat. Their faces, beneath unfriendly, religious hats, were those of farmers, and I thought as I watched them how swiftly they would be 'up to' all the tricks of a peasant parish. As they tramped the deck in sombre conversation, their thick boots seemed separated only by sanctity from boots that follow a plough. Two nuns sat close together as though for mutual protection, wearing that expression, common to all nuns who travel, of having strayed innocently and with folded hands out of some past age. And we were all, for our various reasons, going to Ireland, some of us, no doubt, like myself, for the first time.

Killeney Bay, Co. Dublin

Next page *Dun Laoghaire*

7

I felt rather like the fool of the party because I was bound on perhaps the most stupid and thankless task which a man can set for himself: I was going to add another book to that mountain of books about Ireland. Other people were going merely to fish, to play golf, to look at the old home or to rebuke the sinner. But I was on much more difficult and dangerous ground, and well I knew it.

In order to refrain from brooding and also to satisfy a natural curiosity, I explored the steerage, which was, I discovered, more interesting than the upper regions of this ship. Here were hearty young Irishmen drinking too much at a bar. They were excited. They were full of good humour. One of them told me that he was a barman in the Edgware Road.

There were also many young maids with vivid eyes, highly-strung girls, voluble and un-English. They were also on holiday, or going home to spend a week with mother before they satisfied the Irish urge to move on to some distant land. The men stood together at the bar and the girls sat together apart. Now and then one of the men would carry over a small glass of port and make some gallant remark which would send the girls into peals of laughter:

'Get along with ye, Mick,' cried a big, dark-eyed wench. 'I'll be telling your mother about your goings-on in Hyde Park, I will now . . .'

And everybody roared with laughter. It was all very friendly.

On deck again, I leaned over the rail and looked towards Ireland. What was it going to be like? I was eager and excited.

What little did I know about Ireland?

The Irishmen I had met during the War had resembled the Englishmen unless they were drunk, when they became either intensely violent and smashed camp furniture or in-

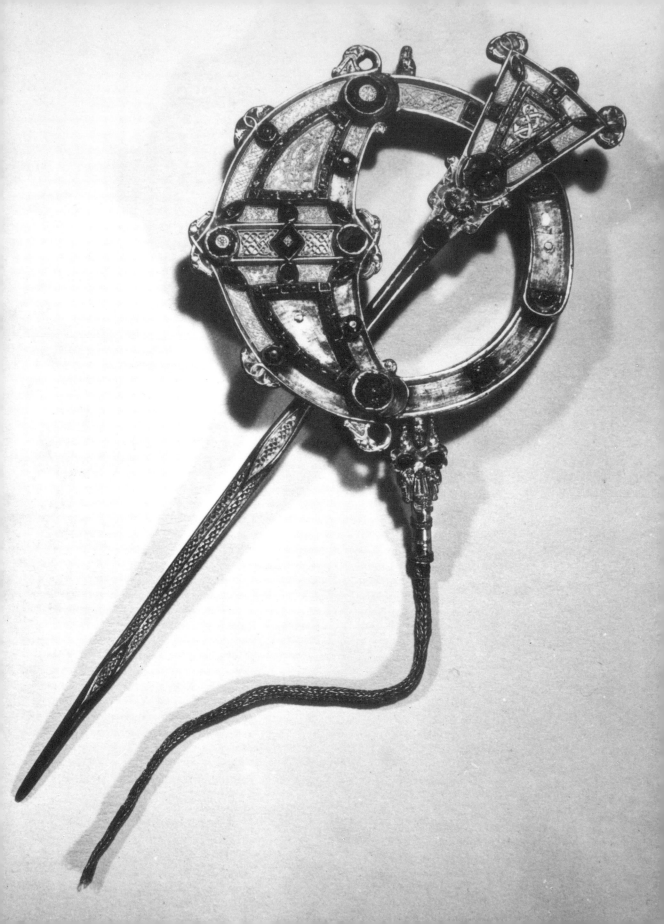

credibly pathetic, which was harder to bear. In such moments they lost an English accent and lapsed into a faint brogue, using words which I suppose they had learnt in childhood from gamekeepers and grooms. When you put them to bed you were never quite sure whether they would try to hit you or kiss you. Sometimes they would try to hit you first and kiss you afterwards.

Many of these good fellows, and they were a hearty, generous slap-dash type, had their creameries and their country houses burnt out in the Rebellion of 1916, which was the first inkling I received – for few Englishmen read Irish history – that Irishmen were of two kinds: the Irishmen of English descent, generally Protestants and officers, and the Irishmen of Irish descent, generally Catholics and sometimes sergeants. Although the Protestant officers would have been infuriated had you called them English – and, in fact, had been known in the splendour of their cups to cry 'To hell with England!' – the Catholic sergeants considered them to be a kind of English, which was very confusing to anyone brought up in the easy English tradition that bygones should be bygones.

Then came that time, the Rebellion of 1916, when Ireland's army (few Englishmen know that she gave 250,000 men to the Services) was hissed through the streets of France with the cry of 'Shinners' and 'Traitors', a pretty cruel moment for them.

I was aware that the time has come when England must look at Ireland in a new light.

I was going not to the land of clowns and 'bulls', which amused the ruling class of two centuries, but to a small country that has stood to its guns through a consistent War of Independence that dragged its weary, blood-stained way through nine centuries – the longest struggle in the history of the world.

Before me on the sky-line was the Irish Free State.

A rim of land grew clearer, and slowly the Wicklow Hills shouldered their way out of the sea. My first impression of them was that they were foreign hills. They were not like any hills in England or Scotland, and it was difficult to say why. The light was, perhaps, different over them; even the clouds seemed to be Irish clouds.

Dunleary – or Dun Laoghaire – which used to be called Kingstown, was an interesting contrast to these foreign hills. Here was an old-fashioned English port with an old-fashioned English railway station.

Dublin in the early morning, with the sun shining, is a city the colour of claret. The red-brick Georgian mansions, with fine doors, fanlights, and little iron balconies at the first-floor windows, stand back in well-bred reticence against wide roads, quiet and dignified, as if the family had just left by stage-coach. Dublin shares with Edinburgh the air of having been a great capital.

This city is as completely a creation of the eighteenth century as Bath. It is a superb, indolent aristocrat among cities, with an easy manner and a fine air of unstudied elegance. The Liffey, crossed by eight bridges, some of them good-looking, cuts the city into a north and south division, and there is pervading Dublin that subtle something as vivid and distinctive as the feel of ships and docks, due to the nearness of great mountains. Just behind Dublin the long, smooth Wicklow Hills lie piled, clear-cut against the sky, brown-green in

13

colour, and from them on clear days, I am told, a man can see across the Irish Sea to the mountains of Wales.

One of the first things that charmed me, as it must charm all visitors, is the Irish voice. The Irish do not like the 'Dublin accent', but it is not so much a matter of accent as of intonation. I found myself listening to people in the street. The cadence of the Irish voice is catching. The habit of giving a little upward kick to the end of a sentence is a charming habit; in women it is adorable.

Why has Dublin been called 'dear dirty Dublin'? This surely is an ancient libel. The roads outside Dublin are apparently dirty on the evidence of the omnibus wheels, to which are attached small hanging brooms of stiff bristles. These brooms tickle the tyres when the wheels are in motion and brush off the mud. But the city itself is as clean as a Dutch dresser.

The crowds in the Dublin streets are vastly different from English crowds. You do not see the haggard money look which is becoming characteristic of all large English cities. There is more laughter. There is no painful rushing about. There is a cheerful ease about Dublin, a casual good temper, which makes it difficult to realize the dark times through which this city has passed. There are certain apparent super-ficialities which, however, possess a deep significance. The English red has vanished from the streets; the pillar-boxes are green. So are the envelopes in which telegrams are delivered. So are the mail vans. And the names of the streets are written in Gaelic.

It must be impossible to be alone in Dublin. The Irish have a genius for improvisation and – they hate to be alone! A man may meet a friend casually in a bus in Dublin at noon and find

15

himself saying good-bye to this man at 3 a.m., having visited together during the night several houses where they have been sincerely welcomed as an interesting conversational turn, much as one might welcome a couple of strolling players.

The hospitality of Dublin is almost embarrassing to an English visitor. If a stranger knows one person he soon knows hundreds. They open their houses to him and let him find his way about. There can be no other capital in the world more generous in its welcome or more devastating in its disapproval. For through Irish life and conversation there runs a bitter spitefulness that at first puzzles you until you understand that it is a national gift. A Catholic bishop once told Padraic Colum that spite and envy are the Catholic vices – the other side of the Catholic virtue of equality – just as harsh individualism and snobbery are the Protestant vices. There may be something in this, in spite of the fact that these vices seem to me shared in equal parts by Catholics and Protestants! But it is a fact that the Irish have a genius for satire. When they get together they love to tell stories that reveal those whom they admire, or those who are important and prominent, in a rather cruelly amusing and belittling light. It is rather confusing at first.

What is George Moore's *Hail and Farewell* and James Joyce's *Ulysses* but this Irish gift for satire that always borders on the malicious?

A stranger lost in the confusing maze of Irish conversation feels at first that nothing is sacred to these people until, finding himself outside in the small hours in company with a man who has been sparkling all evening, he discovers that the former brilliance of his companion has been thrown off as an actor throws off a cloak after a play. The amusing Touchstone of the evening

becomes a sombre Hamlet. As he walks through the empty street he contradicts everything he has previously said in a voice that comes out from him drenched in an abysmal melancholy.

You then realize that talk in Ireland is a game with no rules.

In the cold light of morning you wonder why it sounded so brilliant!

Hamlet came on the following day to say that he would show me the most interesting sight in Dublin.

'We are,' he explained, 'going to see Dáil Eireann which, as you may know, is the Parliament of the Free State.'

The Dáil meets in a large eighteenth-century house, formerly the residence of the Dukes of Leinster. In front of it is a statue of Queen Victoria, which, while not complimentary, is not so bad as the one that sits so heavily on Manchester.

'That,' explained my friend, pointing to the statue, 'is known with justice as "Ireland's Revenge".'

The entrance to the Dáil is like that to any big London club. Members enter, smoking pipes and cigarettes, collect their letters from a porter's box on the right, and go on through Grosvenor Square galleries and up wide ducal stairways to the 'House'.

The Free State Parliament meets in the old lecture theatre of the Royal Dublin Society, which was founded in 1731 for the purpose of promoting useful arts and sciences. The gallery has recently been altered and fitted with protective railings to prevent the accidental fall of spectators or other objects on the deputies' heads, but the floor of the theatre has been fitted with shining mahogany seats, which rise in tiers in a horseshoe round the Speaker's chair. The House is dignified. Beneath the gallery are old prints of Dublin in Hogarth frames.

One's first impression is that immense pains have been taken to introduce as much green into the landscape as possible. Members hold green question papers. When they turn them in unison it is as if a breeze has blown through a forest! The files are green. The note-books are bound in green. Now and then messengers tiptoe down through the seats to deliver emerald green telegrams. At the top of the steps and at the doors stand the most competent-looking chuckers-out seen in public since the heyday of the old music-hall. I would give a man of average physique two seconds to maintain a real row in the Dáil.

An electric bell rang outside in the corridors, members drifted in casually and took their seats. Mr Cosgrave slipped into his place on the Government benches and Dáil Eireann opened as quickly as a directors' meeting when the chairman has to catch a train.

When Mr Guedella looked down on the Dáil he wondered what Mr Gladstone would have thought of 'the last of all his dreams'. And Padraic Colum was inspired by the penetrating thought as he watched Mr Cosgrave that 'the former Irish leaders, even when they were intellectuals like John Dillon, or country gentlemen like John Redmond, all had the air of being chieftains. President Cosgrave looks the magistrate rather than the chieftain, and that contrast lets us know that Irish nationalism is no longer a revolt, a rally, a forlorn hope; it is now an established thing, a directive force: Ireland a Nation has become Ireland a National State.'

As I watched this rather frail-looking man with light-coloured hair that stands up like a cockatoo's crest and light-coloured moustache

and pale eyes, I thought that I had never seen any man who looked less like a rebel. It was difficult to believe not only that this man had suffered in prison for his convictions but that he also possessed the greater courage necessary to steer the government of the Free State through its first years. (I could not forget Griffith, Michael Collins and O'Higgins.) As his even voice, calm and unassuming, went on with the business as though he were controlling a city council I realized that he was the outstanding personality of the Dáil. One looked at Mr de Valera with curiosity but at Mr Cosgrave with respect. He has contributed something new to the conduct of Irish affairs: dignity, calmness, a sense of balance, authority and prestige.

The green question paper of the Dáil is puzzling to a stranger. It is, in slight, innocuous patches, bilingual, but not sufficiently so to baffle a foreigner. Questions to Ministers are addressed first in Irish and then, in case no one can understand them, in English. Irishmen have two names: one in English and one, more difficult to pronounce, in Irish.

Most members prefer to be known in the Dáil by their Gaelic names, so that one comes across in the question paper heroic-sounding names which suggest the battles of giants.

I looked down on the Dáil, thinking that Ireland is never what you expect it to be. I expected eloquence. I expected that some politician would rise up and make me burn with indignation about something. But no; Dáil Eireann was even harder to listen to than the British House of Commons! Where was the Irish wit? Where the Irish pugnacity? Where the sly Irish humour? Where the quick cut and thrust encountered in conversation round the Irish fireside? Where were those amazingly clever things that slip out of an Irishman's mouth before he knows what he has said? They were not in the Dáil! I was surprised that a nation of good talkers could put up such a mumbling show in Parliament.

Then it occurred to me that, of course, they were all very much in earnest. There was nothing playful about them as there is now and then about Westminster. They had fought to get there not only with votes but also with guns. Their Parliament was steeped in the blood of their companions and schoolfellows.

Their voices went on level, solemn, and unemotional, and as I followed my friend downstairs I thought that this was a good omen for Ireland.

The feelings of an unprejudiced Englishman after a first contact with Irish life have been perfectly described by Mr H. W. Nevinson in a preface to one of his fine books. He says that after meeting Irish friends and discussing England with them he feels as though he has been exquisitely operated on for a disease he never had. He was infected by their hatred for the English.

This is so true. The stranger must always be on his guard in case he becomes a too violent Sinn Feiner. There is something extravagant in the air of Ireland which, combined with the engaging and convincing manners of its people, goes right to the heart and sometimes to the head. Many of the greatest Irish nationalists have been English or Anglo-Irish.

The Irish are, of course, sometimes unfair, which, I think, proceeds from the fact that they possess no sense of historical perspective. Even educated Irishmen will talk about Cromwell's campaign as though it was the work of the present British Government. A wrong has never died in Ireland. Every injustice inflicted on Ireland since the time of Strongbow is as real as last year's Budget. No allowance is made for the greater brutality of past centuries, and if you venture to argue about it they bring out the Black and Tans to prove that the 'Saxon' (this is an amusing term) was always a brute.

It sometimes happens that a man is forced to hear the confession of a friend's wife. You may know the man only as a good fellow, sincere, upright, and honest. And the woman tells you that she is suing for divorce on grounds of cruelty. It is difficult to believe it. How is it possible that this fine fellow has knocked this woman about and intimidated her? You listen in horror to her story of mental and physical suffering.

The incompatibility of temperament between England and Ireland affects you in exactly the same way; and you look at the Free State Flag and say:

'Well thank heaven, she got her divorce!'

The history of Ireland is the struggle of the Gael. The old stock was dispossessed but never suppressed. It found an outlet for its resistance even if it had to enlist in foreign armies and intrigue, sometimes hopelessly, in foreign countries. And always behind the hedge in Ireland was there a Mac with a pitch-fork who felt himself to be the real ruler of the land and the scion of kings.

Now for the first time since the Battle of Kinsale the men who control Ireland are the old stock, the O's and the Mac's.

I went to call on a young Irishman who had played a part in the fight for independence. He lives in a small villa in one of the suburbs of Dublin. It is a house with a small front garden and a general air of rectitude quite English. His study was upstairs.

Christ Church Cathedral

'Michael Collins hid here when he was on the run,' he explained.

The houses in Dublin in which Michael Collins sought refuge are as numerous as the English beds in which Queen Elizabeth slept. I wondered as I looked round the ordinary little room whether I was not seeing something which future generations would wish modern Irishmen to preserve.

I shall always regret that I missed Michael Collins by five minutes when he was in London, moving about rather furtively and shyly and refusing to become a social sight, as so many hostesses in Mayfair wished him to be. To produce 'Mick' Collins at a dinner-party was the dream of many a foolish woman's life just before the signing of the Treaty.

This ex-postal clerk was one of those remarkable characters which nations, in moments of good fortune, throw up, frequently in the least likely direction. Although Irishmen do not talk much of him today I believe that future ages may perhaps think of him as the Bonnie Prince Charlie of Ireland. Like Prince Charles Edward he was young, handsome, fearless, and a fugitive. Romance will in the generosity of time claim him. But, unlike Charles Edward, he was successful and he died, as Charles should have died on Culloden Moor, before times of peace could ruin a reputation gained in war. The only fortunate warriors are those who are lucky enough to perish in the moment of victory.

I have talked to many English soldiers and to many journalists who acted as special correspondents during the 'Trouble' – most of whom, by the way, had sympathy with Sinn Fein – and I have never heard anything but admiration for the military skill and the personal courage of Michael Collins.

The stranger passing through the gates of Trinity College beneath the gaze of Burke and Goldsmith finds himself on a wide expanse of cobble-stones planted by some ancient humorist to torture the bunions of learned men. Most cities possess a sanctuary which offers, or appears to offer, an escape from everyday things, and, like the Temple in London and Cheetham's Hospital in Manchester, such places become more impressive when they lie in the very heart of the city. This is so with Trinity College. You pass through its gates into a rather thoughtful world.

Trinity College is the only monument to the Elizabethan age in Dublin.

It has always been criticized as a stronghold of the Protestant intruder, and I am told that during the 1916 Rebellion letters were intercepted which referred to it as 'the foreign college'.

Every visitor to Dublin should go to Trinity to see one of the most precious books in existence – the famous Book of Kells. This book is taken from its case every evening and locked in a safe in the vaults; every morning it is carried reverently to its glass-case again, and one leaf is turned each day. What is the value of the Book of Kells? Many men have wondered. Professors have been known to speculate in the sanctity of the family circle how much it would mean a year if Trinity sold the beastly book and devoted the proceeds to the staff! (This, of course, is an Irish joke!)

The value of the Book of Kells is the sum which one millionaire, bidding against another millionaire, would pay at Sotheby's for it. This depends, in its turn, on the depth of hatred and rivalry between them. Both of them might think they had won, for instance, if the price was

Georgian Dublin

£500,000!* And the Book of Kells is not insured! There can be no other book of its character in the world which is not insured. The college authorities, and no doubt wisely, feel that money could not produce another such book, so that the best insurance is to spend a fraction of the premium that would be necessary on extra fire-hoses and watchmen.

I was permitted by the courtesy of the librarian to examine the book. He even allowed me to turn one of its thick vellum pages.

What is the Book of Kells?

When the barbarian was exploring the ruins of Roman cities in England and the imported gods howled for blood along the sea-coast of Norfolk, Irish monks decided to set sail for England and bear into that distressful country the light of Christian learning.

London at this time was a haunted Roman ruin on a hill, with the brambles over London Wall and the camp-fires of the East Angles shining in the marsh beyond the city, which they were afraid to enter; Paris was a desolation, and the sun was setting over Rome. But Armagh, the religious capital of Ireland, was the centre of European culture. During the three darkest centuries of English history, Ireland was saving Greek and Latin culture for Europe. It was from Ireland, by way of Iona and Lindisfarne, that sandy little island off the Northumbrian coast, that Christianity came to the north of England.

At the beginning of this time an unknown Irish monk was writing the Gospels in an abbey at Kells in Meath, founded by St Columba. He was one of the world's greatest artists. In Italy of the Renaissance he might have been another Michael Angelo.

*Editor's note: No attempt has been made to adjust 1929 prices to the present day.

He enriched his book with a thousand fantasies and a thousand beauties of intricate design. He poured into this book all the power of his imagination. Men looking at it today wonder not only at the fertility of his brain but also at the keenness of his eyes. How is it possible that a man, unless he employed a type of magnifying glass unknown in his day, could pen such microscopic designs, so perfect that sections of them no larger than a postage stamp when photographed and enlarged show no flaw in the intricate interlocking of lines and spirals?

This great relic of Irish art was placed in a costly gold shrine. Later in history a thief stole it from the sacristy of the Abbey of Kells. It was found two months afterwards hidden in the earth. The thief had taken it for the shrine; and so the book, flung carelessly away, was recovered, and remains the most perfect expression of Christian art which has survived from the Golden Age of Ireland.

It is in the Book of Kells that Ireland's remote past lives gloriously in subtle line and perfect colour. When a man turns the pages of that great book he turns back the centuries to a world of Irish saints, of Irish poems, of Irish legends, of Irish boats sailing over the sea taking the light of the Christian Church into the dark places of the world.

The Book of Kells and the 'Gold Room' in Dublin's remarkable museum must astonish those who do not know the position occupied by this country from A.D. 600 to about A.D. 800.

If there is an Englishman who believes that early Ireland was as savage as Anglo-Saxon England, let him go to the 'Gold Room' – one of the most interesting rooms in Dublin – and examine the beaten gold torcs, the shining lunulae, the jewelled shrines, the metal croziers, the exquisite cups and vases, all stamped with a vigorous art and a stern convention as different from anything known to us as the art of Egypt differs from that of Greece.

I think that one of the most exquisite things in Dublin is the Tara brooch. It was found on the beach near Bettystown, near Drogheda, in 1850. There is no connexion between this brooch and Tara. The name was given to it by the jeweller into whose possession it came. It is a bronze pin shaped like a Roman fibula. It is decorated with panels in fine gold filigree work, enamel, amber and glass. It is as characteristic as the Book of Kells. It is decorated at the back and the front with every form of Celtic ornamentation: spirals, interlacing, human heads and zoomorphic decorations.

The verger of Christ Church Cathedral – which is one of Dublin's three cathedrals – loves to take a stranger down into the ghostly crypt, which is said to have been built by the Danes in the time when Sigtrygg Silkbeard was King of Dublin. In this cold spot, where the electric light serves only to increase the gloom of the arches which spring from a forest of stunted pillars, are the roots of Dublin.

When this crypt was built there were men alive who remembered the Homeric battle of Clontarf, and how the great battle-axe of Prince Murragh, the eldest son of Brian Boru, rose and fell dripping red in the fight as he headed his Dalcassians against 1,000 picked Norsemen clad in chain armour. Perhaps the very men whose hands placed these stones one upon the

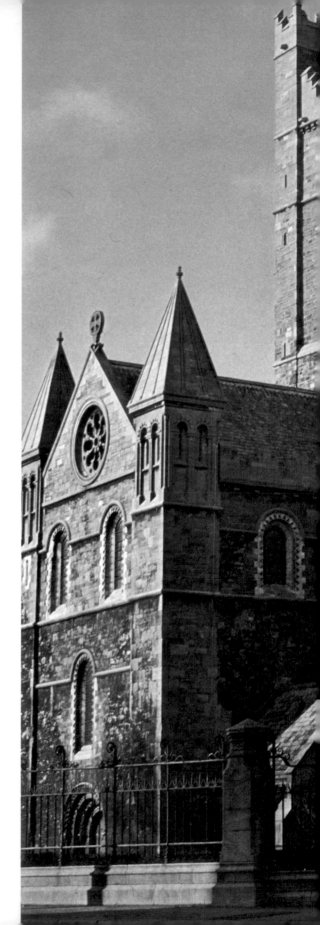

other had seen the fight that swayed round the tent of Brian when it became known that Brodur the sea king had rushed in and killed the aged monarch as he knelt in prayer, giving God thanks for victory.

Christ Church was built twenty-four years after the battle of Clontarf. Between that time and the building of the crypt the Kingdom of Ireland relapsed again into petty States, and history is a mist that blows aside for a moment now and then, to show us the long-boats of the Danes beached on the east coast of Ireland, battles, defeats, victories, and, at length, a little Danish settlement on Dublin Bay.

The verger takes you up into the church, and you see a fine Norman transept, and, not far away, in the nave lies the body of a stone Crusader in full armour. This is the tomb of Strongbow. With him Ireland's troubles began. He held Dublin for Henry II, and founded the Irish problem.

Some memory of Strongbow's ruthlessness lingers on at least in the mind of the verger of Christ Church. He tells you how Strongbow broke his way in through Dublin wall, slaughtering and pillaging. Then he points to a small stone effigy that lies beside the Norman. It is that of a young boy, but it is cut off at the waist.

'And do ye not know who that is?' asked the verger, leading up dramatically to the information. 'That's the son of Strongbow. He was only a lad, and his father said he had shown fear in the battle, so he killed him and cut his body in two as a warning to all cowards. That's the kind of man, a cruel, hard man, he was entirely. . . . Now come this way and I'll show ye the heart of St Laurence O'Toole.'

He points to a heart-shaped metal case, the size of a cushion, chained and padlocked to the

wall. In this case is the heart of the famous Laurence O'Toole, Archbishop of Dublin, who died in Normandy in 1180.

But of all the mysteries, grotesque and historic, locked away in Christ Church, I think the verger's special pride is the statue of an orphan, down whose cheek runs a stone tear. He lights a match and holds it near the statue.

'Do you see it?' he asks.

It is, I suppose, a greater marvel to his visitors than the grim and terrible memories called up by the church that was founded by Sigtrygg Silkbeard. . . .

In St Patrick's Cathedral, nearby, you come with something of a shock to the graves of Swift and Stella, together at last in death. You have to search for that famous epitaph, hard and bitter as its author, which no one but Swift could have written. It was removed from his tomb many years ago, and is now to be seen over the door of the robing-room:

*Here lies the Body of
Jonathan Swift,
for thirty years dean
of this cathedral,
where savage indignation can
no longer gnaw his heart.
Go, traveller, and
imitate, if you can, one who
played a man's part in defence
of Liberty.*

Those words have gone round the world. And how poor and commonplace in comparison are those not far away which commemorate Stella.

There are many things to be seen in St Patrick's – the flags of the disbanded Irish regiments, the stall of the Knights of St Patrick, and a number of fine memorials – but always one returns to the two stones in the nave which cover the bodies of the two most mysterious lovers in English literature.

Stout is a drink which in some mysterious way has become wedded to the oyster. It is the robust and slightly heavier brother of beer. Most men like it, and thin women drink it as a duty. We are constantly told that 'it is good for us'.

This dark and satisfying fluid is occasionally mixed by those of exotic taste with port or sherry, producing a drink which is famed as a 'corpse reviver'.

Dublin is the home of stout. Guinness's brewery is the world's largest brewery, and it is, speaking industrially, Dublin. It is the greatest employer of labour in the Irish capital, and the only firm with a world-wide reputation. A jet black river of Guinness trickles into every corner of the thirsty world, taking with it the name of Dublin.

When I went there to learn the mysteries of stout I entered a walled city devoted to drink. There are railway lines in it, and a canal on which sail barges with cargoes from all the barley fields of Ireland.

Now and then these barges, which are a distinctive feature of the landscape, draw from loungers on the banks the ironic shout:

'Will ye bring us back a parrot?'

The recipe for stout is simple: it is hops (Kentish and Californian mixed), pale malt, and a certain quantity of roast malt or barley. Roast malt looks exactly like coffee, which explains the Ethiopian colour of the 'wine of Ireland'.

Now, the first ordeal endured by potential Guinness is that of the brew-house, in which it is, after mixing, drawn off as a thin, sweet, coffee-like liquid known as 'wort'. The 'wort' is next boiled with hops and pumped through long pipes into the fermenting house.

Yeast is added to assist fermentation, and as you look through a door you see this khaki-coloured scum moving in a slow, repulsive manner, opening and closing a bubbly eye here and there with a kind of obscene intelligence.

The brewery joke is to take a visitor to these vats, and wait for that inevitable moment when he puts his head over them to see better. Then, with the speed of an electric shock, something far superior to the world's worst smell leaps out and hits him in the face. It is not a smell: it is a gas. If a man were held in this gas for five seconds he could not breathe, and if for ten he would be dead.

Every visitor to the brewery ends up in the tasting-room, where the choicest vintage is ready for him. A wise man drinks only one tankard of that mysterious beverage known as 'foreign extra'. This is a stout of liqueur-like potency which has matured for five or seven years. It is designed for foreign consumption, and it is said that it reconciles exiles all over the world to the sadness of their fate. The kick of a full-grown mule is in each bottle.

'Och!' said my guide, 'they call it the drink of heaven!'

I am sure that is not a good name for it.

The joke in this room is to give the visitor two bottles of 'foreign extra' and then watch him walk to the gate.

The most gruesome sight I have encountered in any city is to be seen beneath the Church of St Michan, in Dublin.

St Michan is said to have been a Danish bishop who founded a church in the year A.D. 1095, above vaults built on the site of an ancient oak forest. The church was rebuilt on town-hall lines during the eighteenth century. The only objects of interest contained in it are a Stool of Repentance, a pulpit which at one time could be swung round to face any section of the congregation, and a good-looking organ, sprouting gilded cherubs, on which Handel, so they say, practised his 'Messiah' before the first performance in Dublin.

Visitors go to St Michan's to look at the bodies in the vaults beneath. These are preserved by some peculiarity of the atmosphere as perfectly as Egyptian mummies. Morbid persons, and those who like to feel their flesh creeping, will find it worthwhile to visit Dublin to see this awful place, because it is unique in Ireland; and there is certainly nothing like it in England. I seem to remember once seeing rows of mummified monks in the crypt of a church at Bonn, on the Rhine, but, unless my memory is at fault, they were skeletons compared with the mummies of St Michan's.

The sexton takes you outside through the churchyard and approaches heavy iron doors on the ground level against the wall of the church. These he unlocks, and you look down a steep flight of stone steps into the darkness of the charnel-house. You notice as you descend that the air is not the chilled, clammy air of a crypt: it is almost warm, and of a surprising freshness.

'This,' says the sexton, as he goes down before you, 'is the best air in Dublin.'

A number of high-vaulted cells lead off from each side of a central passage running east and west beneath the church. They are fitted with iron gates. The sexton takes an electric lamp, opens a gate, and, leading the way into one of the vaults, flashes his torch over the most ghastly sight you can imagine.

Coffins lie stacked one on top of another almost to the roof. You are in the vault of a noble family. Lords and ladies, generals and statesmen, known and unknown, lie round you in human strata. The last coffin placed in

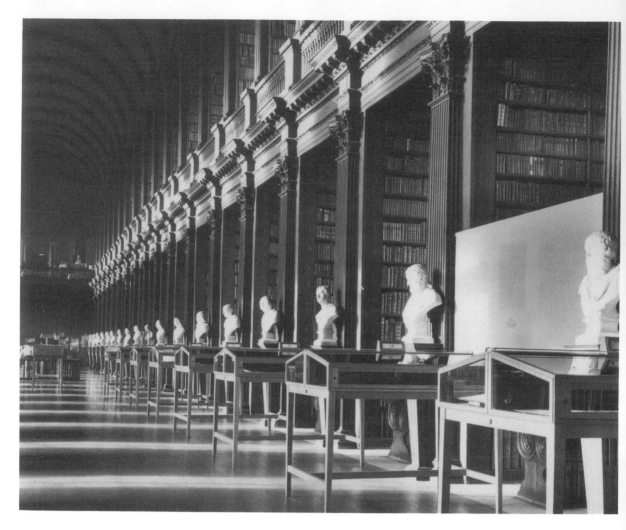

position rests on others, which in their turn rest on that of the great-great-grandfather. The lower coffins are of a shape and colour long out-dated. Some, which bear coats-of-arms, are covered in red velvet, which has not decayed much or faded in colour; others are bound in black leather, and are studded with big brass nails which have not tarnished.

When you look more closely you notice that the weight of the dead pressing on the dead has caused the coffins to collapse into one another, exposing here a hand, there an arm, a leg, or a head. The idea of dead men pushing their ancestors from their coffins is worthy of Edgar Allan Poe. But what does startle and horrify is that these men and women, many of whom have been dead for 500 years and more, have not gone back to the dust; they are like mummies, their flesh is the texture of tough leather, and, stranger still, their joint bones work.

'Look!' said the sexton, moving a knee, anxious that I should miss nothing.

In a corner I saw the body of a man lying with one leg crossed over the other, the traditional death posture of a Crusader. This indicated that he had been to the Holy Land. You can see this position sculptured in stone on the tombs in the Temple Church, London, and in thousands of other Norman memorials up and down England, but I never thought it possible to see the Crusader himself.

'You can shake hands with him!' said the sexton. I bent down and examined the nails of a man who had been dead for nearly 800 years.

In the same vault is the body of a woman, said to be a nun, whose feet and right hand have been amputated. The story is that she was tortured and mutilated hundreds of years ago.

We went into many other vaults, notably that of a family which has died out. This place was a

The north side of the Long Room, Trinity College. There is no artificial light in the Long Room, which is closed at dusk.

nightmare. Intimate fragments of this family were lying about the floor in a thin brown dust of decayed coffins.

The only living creatures in these vaults are spiders. In certain places they have spun thin grey shrouds from roof to floor. In one vault they have made a merciful curtain over the door.

'What do they live on?'

'Themselves,' says the sexton. 'Men who study spiders come here from all over the place, and I have been told that spiders are cannibals. . . .'

The generally accepted theory, which explains the remarkable preservative quality of the vaults, is that the air is chemically impregnated by the remains of the oak forest which stood there in ancient times. So long as the vaults are kept perfectly dry decay ceases. Let only a little moisture enter, then bodies and coffins crumble into fine dust. When the two brothers, John and Henry Sheares, who were beheaded in the eighteenth century, were re-coffined in 1853 – they used to stand upright in a vault with their heads beside their feet – the people of Dublin brought wreaths and flowers to the vault. The moisture in these flowers wrecked everything in the vault within a year.

I was glad to reach the cold air and the daylight.

'Do you show these vaults to women?' I asked.

'I always warn ladies,' he said, 'or I'd be having them fainting on me. . . . I'll not forget the first time I came here fourteen years ago, and me not knowing a thing about it at all. I took a candle – there was no electric light then – and went down to have a look. I got the biggest fright of my life. . . .

'Yes, they do tell a ghost story about it. It's about a thief who went down one dark night to take a ring from a lady's finger, and, as he was working away, the lady sat up in her coffin and stepped out over the side and walked away. Yes, she did! And they say she lived for years after. But that's all blarney, sir. . . .'

St Michan's is Dublin's chamber of horrors!

It occurred to me at about three o'clock one morning that I must tear myself away from the terrible friendliness of Dublin and see Ireland. I knew that I could not face all my sudden friends and say:

'I am going away at once!'

They would have replied:

'But what's the hurry? Come on now and we'll go and see So-and-so!'

And I would have been flattered, swayed, and conquered. So I made secret arrangements for a motor-car, wrote a lot of apologies, and early one morning escaped from Dublin like a criminal.

2
WICKLOW TO CORK

It was a warm summer morning and the dew still on the grass when I took the road over the hills.

No such wilderness as the Dublin hills lies at the door of any great city. The Peak District, at the back door of Sheffield, is tame compared with the miles of melancholy peat bog which never has given, and never will give, food or shelter to man.

You could be lost in the hills within an hour of Dublin; you could wander for days without meeting a soul; you could, if injured, lie there and die in the bog because your chance of finding help would be indeed remote.

The great hills, more savage even than Dartmoor, lie fold on fold, some long and of gentle outline, others sharp and conical; and in their hollows you come unexpectedly to deep lakes such as Lough Dan, lying like a patch of fallen sky. Little brown streams trickle through the peat. The whole landscape is a study in various browns; brown peat like dark chocolate; black brown water; light brown grass; dark brown pyramids of cut peat stacked at intervals along the brown road.

But in the evening the hills turn blue. White mists rise in the hollows and lie there like thin veils hung from hill to hill. The sun sets. And there is no sound but the wind blowing through the tough grass and the thin trickle of water running to the valleys.

A man might be among the dead mountains of the moon.

The Avoneberg River, Glenmalure, Co. Wicklow

Next page *Slea Head and Blasket Islands, Dingle Peninsular, Co. Kerry*

So I have come into Wicklow, where the fields
are sharply green, where a wild beauty hides in
the glens, where sudden surprising vistas open
up as the road rises and falls; and here I smell
for the first time the incense of Ireland, the
smoke of turf fires, and here for the first time I
see the face of the Irish countryside.

It is not an easy, comfortable countryside like
that of England. It has not the same settled
confidence. It has a strange and foreign look. I
feel at times that I am in France. No half-
timbered cottages stand rooted in the soil
wearing thatches like old hats; no cosy inns call
themselves 'The Nag's Head' or 'The Fox and
Hounds'.

There are instead small one-storey houses
of stone, whitewashed so that they hurt the eyes
as they shine in the sun. Some are so small that
a child might think them the houses of fairies.
Often a full-sized Irish face looks out from a
window no bigger than a table-napkin. All these
houses standing against the road have little
green doors designed for contemplation. It is
possible to make half-doors of them on which a
thoughtful man may lean and smoke his pipe
and watch the world go past, just as if he were
leaning on the rail of a ship.

When these doors are open I can see into the
half dusk of a room in which a small red flame
burns before a shrine.

In a field nearby a farmer stands among his
herds, a pipe in his mouth, a stick in his hand,
and an eye on the main road; his wife sets out
towards the next town leading a small donkey
in a small cart. And down the country roads of
Ireland walk some of the best-looking country
girls in the world. Some are small and red-faced,
with dark eyes; others are fair and freckled
about the nose, with blue eyes. They possess
great dignity of bearing.

I saw a hatless girl carrying a basket on one arm and on the other a baby wrapped in the fold of a black shawl. There was nothing of the peasant in her appearance. She had a fine face and thoroughbred ankles.

A man cannot go far along an Irish road without meeting a horseman. Often a priest talks to a young farmer who leans slightly from the saddle and pats his horse while he replies to 'his riv'rence', and the horse is not the English farmer's nag; there is blood in him.

I miss flowers in cottage gardens. I go through village after village thinking that if I were an Irishman I would start a society for the planting of them in little gardens all over the land. But most of all I miss that triumph of the English landscape – the village Inn.

There is, it is true, in every town a drink saloon called after the name of past or present owner, 'Casey's' or 'Dempsey's', dull and ugly buildings, so strange and uncouth in a country noted for its sociability and its good manners. Outside at thirsty moments of the day gather numerous gigs, traps, jaunting-cars, and sometimes a shaggy little donkey and cart.

But over it all – the white houses, the green fields with their stone walls, the long road winding, the slow herds coming along in the knee-deep dust, the sweet smell of turf burning, the little carts with coloured shafts, the soft Irish voices, the quick Irish smiles – over it all, and in it as if imprisoned in the stone and brick of this country, as if buried beneath the grass and hidden in the trees, is something that is half magic and half music.

There is something in a minor key that a man never quite hears. Perhaps no stranger ever hears it. But I think the Irish do. It is something drawn up out of the earth of Ireland, out of the water in the streams and the grass and flowers in the fields, something of the sky and of the earth – a something that is mysterious and like a fall of dew over the land.

What it is I shall probably never know. It is what people mean when they say that Ireland 'gets you' or that Ireland is 'fascinating'.

It is something subtle and deeply rooted and very old, something that may be the blessing or the curse of Ireland. If you could translate it into sound I imagine it would be rather like the twittering of a fiddle.

I am sure that this minor note which just escapes the ear is important. If a man could hear it he would know nearly all there is to know about Ireland.

I have stood on the windy sands of Lindisfarne, where St Cuthbert made his cell, and on that hill in Somerset where, so they say, St Joseph of Arimathea planted the Holy Thorn, but no place has given me a clearer picture of early Christianity than the strange little ruined city of Glendalough, in Co. Wicklow.

I do not think Ireland can have anything more lovely to show than this heavenly little valley, with its two small lakes lying cupped in a hollow of the hills. So high are the hills and so deep the lakes that even on a sunny day the waters are still and black.

A tall, round tower rises above the trees at the lakeside, one of those towers peculiar to Ireland, and built nearly 1,000 years ago as a belfry and a refuge from the Danes. The doors are high up in these towers, so that refugees could pull up the ladder after them and feel secure from attack.

Round the tower, lost in trees, covered in green moss and tangled in brambles, or perched

Mountain stream, Co. Wicklow

The Round Tower, Glendalough, Co. Wicklow

high on ledges of the cliffs, are the ruins of a religious community which was established centuries before England was a Christian country.

The bells rang for Mass in Glendalough when there was no sound in England but the meeting of the sword on sword and the cries of the Vikings beaching their ships.

I sat on a bridge over a brown, troutful stream, watching two boys approach leading a donkey laden with wood in panniers. They promised to send the boatman to me, so that I could go over the lake and climb to St Kevin's Bed.

St Kevin was the founder of Glendalough. He came to it about the year 520 – was there one Christian in England at that date? – to lead a hermit's life.

There is an ancient tradition, the source of a thousand songs and poems, that he was driven into solitude by the passion of a beautiful girl named Kathleen, who favoured him with relentless ardour. The old chronicle states that 'the holy youth rejected all these allurements'.

One day finding the young monk alone in the fields, she approached him and clasped him in her arms. 'But the soldier of Christ, arming himself with the sacred sign and full of the Holy Ghost, made strong resistance against her, and rushed out of her arms into the wood, and finding nettles, took secretly a bunch of them and struck her with them many times in the face, hands, and feet. And when she was blistered with the nettles, the pleasure of her love became extinct.'

So says legend. Another version, exploited by the poet Moore, is that St Kevin, in order to rid himself of his fair admirer, pushed her into the lake!

The historic fact remains that the young hermit retired to Glendalough, where he lived at first in a hollow tree and later in a small cave which he discovered high up in the sheer face of the cliff.

Disciples came from near and far. Gradually there grew up round the lake a little sanctuary of holy men. St Kevin lived to see his disciples go out from Glendalough to found schools and monasteries in other parts of Ireland. This little ruined city – an Irish Thebaid – was a school of Irish saints.

'Good evening, sir.'

I looked up and saw the boatman standing before me.

'And it's the saint's bed ye'll be seeing this evening?' he asked. 'Wait now while I get the boat out. . . . Step aisy, now!'

As we went over the still, dark water and he told me the story of St Kevin and his struggle with the ardent Kathleen I asked him if it was true that the saint pushed her into the lake.

'Begor,' he said, 'and what kind of a saint would he be to treat a young lady like that? The truth of it is that he bothered her with nettles, and she was cured of her love and became a nun. Now, sir, look back there!'

He pursed up his mouth and looked solemn, as his type does before 'putting over' a bit of blarney: 'On that stone Kathleen appears every night at ten. I've seen her with me own eyes, that I have, and the loveliest creature that ever stepped she is.'

'How deep is the lake?'

'It's that deep, sir, that my sister went bathing there a while back and sank. . . .' He paused solemnly, and added, 'We heard not a word from her until we got a letter from Manchester asking us to post her some dry clothes. That's how deep it is, sir.'

I knew that the man was acting up to a tradition established by centuries of tourists. He was expected to talk like this and to tell tall stories; and I could not help admiring him because he did it so well.

St Kevin's Bed – the cell in which the saint lived before the 'Seven Churches' were built – is high up in the cliff. It is a perilous climb, but thousands do it every year. Once in the cave you can sit down and contemplate the waters and wonder how on earth you are going to get down again.

It is seven o'clock in the morning. The air is like iced wine. The sun is brighter over the Curragh, which is the Salisbury Plain of Ireland. Clouds are vast above it, and far off on the sky the Dublin mountains lie in a blue mist, fold on fold.

My horse throws up his head and fidgets to fling himself through the morning over the green grass; and I hold him in, loving his impatience and the shining life in him which is something pure and classic from the beginning of the world. I pat his neck and whisper to him, denying him cruelly, telling him to be patient.

'Let me go,' he seems to say. 'Let me match the beauty of my strength with the beauty of the world!'

'Go, go – *now*!' I press my knees lightly to him; and, with a kind of elemental ecstasy, he springs forward into the sunlight; and – I forget everything but the rush of the wind, the rhythm of his hoof-beats on the turf, and the heady joy of riding a horse in the early morning.

The whole bright world rushes towards us. I see a gleam of snow-white rails above the grass; the deserted Curragh Racecourse. But the plain is awake. It is dotted with racehorses at exercise or gallops. This place is a nursery of racehorses, the finest in the world. As I pass them trotting, walking, galloping, I wish that I had an Irishman with me to say to me in a reverent whisper:

'There goes so and so who sired many a winner!'

To the men of the Curragh these horses are the local heroes. The spirit of the Curragh is a lightly-stepping thoroughbred – fetlocks in brown bandages – the very incarnation of nervous energy, speed, and breeding.

I come into the little town of Kildare. It is shuttered and asleep in the early morning, save for a drover and his kine. There is a sudden great clatter of horses, and round the corner, riding one and leading one, comes a squadron of Free State cavalry at early morning exercise. The years drop from me, and I follow them longingly with my eyes fancy following an early morning parade longingly! – as they go at a heavy jog-trot down the hill towards the miles of open country.

As I follow slowly I hear behind me the sound of hoofs, but very different from the hearty clatter of a cavalry squadron. It is a delicate, nervous, lady-like sound, and, turning, I see a string of racehorses. There are sixteen of them. Beauties!

A stable-boy walks at the head of each holding a white band attached to the head collar. Each horse wears knee-caps and fetlock bandages. Following the long file comes a dogcart containing a man who looks at the horses with the expression of a mother. He is the manager of a stud farm watching the stately procession of a year's hard work and devotion.

These horses are yearlings. They are as nervous as kittens. The very sound of their

shoes on the road startles them. To pass from sunlight into a tree shadow causes them to sidestep and fling up their lovely narrow heads.

'They are going to the yearling sales at Newmarket,' says the man in the dogcart. 'And a better batch of yearlings has never left the Curragh. Poor little devils! They don't know what's up this morning! This is the first time they've been on the roads. See that filly, the fourth from the end, she's worth ten thousand pounds if she's worth a penny! I reckon there's seventy thousand pounds' worth of horseflesh in front of us this morning. . . .

'Yes; it's an anxious job taking yearlings to England. We have a special train, then the boat to Holyhead, and a special train to Newmarket. But yearlings don't understand travel. An experienced old racehorse will lean against the box in the train and rest himself, and he'll let himself go with the rise and fall of a ship; but, bless you, yearlings are just little children! They knock themselves about in the train and panic on the boat. It takes pounds off their weight.

'Why is the Curragh so famous for horse-breeding?'

'It's a limestone plain, and the Curragh pasture is the best bone-making country in the world.'

'Is it uniformly good, or does it lie in patches?'

'If you want to make a stud farm here you must prospect for it and choose the best ground, but, having found it, you'll raise up real horses on it.'

The Lakes, Blessington, Co. Wicklow

Above *Carrick-on-Suir Castle, Co. Tipperary*

St Kevin's Church, Glendalough

Next page *An inlet near Glandore, Co. Cork*

High gold clouds are wheeling above the Curragh. The white racecourse rails sweep round into the green distance. There is a feeling of space, air, birds in the sky; over the green turf of the plain come in long, easy canters men and women on horseback and small children in corduroy breeches astride fat ponies. A little encampment of tents has grown up against the white rails. There is a smell of wood smoke and turf. There is a smell of crushed grass. There are booths shining with yellow lemonade and vivid cakes. There are long, crowded canvas bars where men toss down porter or Irish whisky. There are bookies shouting. There are thousands of men and women talking; and the bright light gives a sparkle to it all, flings up the colours so that it might be some fine, shining canvas which contains the essential essence of all race-meetings.

Race-meetings in Ireland seem to attract every eccentric character in the neighbourhood. Ireland is a country of vivid personalities, as England was in the eighteenth and nineteenth centuries before life was influenced by standardization. The individuality of an Irish crowd is stimulating. It is full of vitality. It is full of originality. There is a Hogarthian robustness about it.

An old woman whose matted grey hair escapes from a shawl begs in a gracious voice as soft as light falling through stained glass in a church; and when you give her a coin she pours a benediction over you that, like the gratitude of most Irish beggars, really warms the cockles of your heart. She goes into a booth and taps the drink-wet counter with a coin.

'A glass of whisky if ye plaze. . . .'

The barman regards her with grave disapproval:

'Have I not tould ye, Bridget O'Brien, that if

River Blackwater at Cappoquin, Co. Waterford

Kilkenny

ye drink any more this day it's the police that'll come to ye and lock ye up as they locked ye up at Punchestown?...'

'The polis!' she cries, suddenly abandoning her Madonna-pose and baring her teeth as she leans furiously over the counter, 'the polis!'

The word police seemed to let loose some fury in her.

'Bring them to me,' she cries with extravagant rage. 'There's not a polisman in the land who'll be laying his dirty hands on me this day. Bring them to me!...'

She stands there like some champion offering ordeal by battle.

'Now get along out o' this, will ye?' says the barman soothingly, 'for it's no whisky I've got for ye.'

'To hell wid the polis!' she cries, becoming a raving virago. 'To hell wid them all, I say; and me an O'Brien!'

She shakes her head and glooms. Her wrath falls from her. She has descended into some abysmal pit of sorrow where apparently she communes with the soul of all O'Briens. She looks up with tears in her eyes: an injured aristocrat.

'Och, it's not hard ye'd be on a poor ould woman. Come now, just one glass and it's not troubling ye' I'll be all the day.'

She gazes at the barman as if she had seen him for the first time and discovered something incredible about him.

'And can a handsome, civil young man like yerself turn an ould woman away wid hard words and she asking no more than she can pay for.... Arrah, come on wid ye now and——'

The barman, at the end of all his patience, makes as though he would come round and turn her out. She instantly flares up again.

'To hell wid ye!' she screams, banging her hand on the bar, which is only a trestle-table with oilcloth over it, so that it rebounds under her rage. 'Bad luck on ye and may the divil take ye.... The polis! Is it the polis ye'd bring to me? Is it insulting me ye'd be?'

At this moment a young Civic Guard appears in the opening of the tent. He says nothing. He just stands there. The old woman stabs the barman between the eyes with a glance. It is the glance of a tragedy queen. There is in it anger, dignity, pride, a colossal sense of injury, and a magnificent exaggeration which crops up so often in Irish affairs. She moves over the grass of the tent into the sunlight. The Civic Guard winks at the barman and the barman attacks his arrears of wet glasses.

'It's drunk she'd be if I let her,' he says, 'poor ould divil.... Shure I'm sorry for the poor woman.'

Moving among the crowd is the pitiful figure of old Bridget.

'For the love av God?' she whispers in a voice as soft as the glow of candles.

A more knowing-looking crowd would be impossible to find. You look at it and feel a certain sympathy for the bookmakers. How on earth can they make any money? Their clients are not the usual tipsters who have heard something from the horse's mouth: they *are* the horse's mouth!

What shall I back?

'Wait a while,' says a friend. 'I'll go and see Johnnie and find out if his horse will win.'

He disappears towards the jockeys' and owners' quarters and returns mysteriously, speaking to me from behind his race card in the voice of a conspirator.

'Back Diogenes,' he says.

I go to a bookmaker and discover that there are only four horses in the race. Small fields – even three runners – are common in Ireland. I find that Diogenes is the favourite and I only get two to one.

'Did you back Diogenes?' says my friend.

'I did.'

'Well, you're all right.'

'How do you know?'

'I just know. Hullo, here they come!'

Free State cavalry in green ride slowly down the course opposite the grand-stand and clear it of people. The horses come out in long, easy gallops, the little men with the wind in their coloured silk shirts leaning over their withers; and there is a fine sound of hooves thudding quickly on grass as they go to the post.

The crowd is now quieter. The bookies set up a final clamour.

'They're off!'

The crowd is now silent. The larks are trilling in the sky. The Dublin and the Wicklow hills look quite near in the sharp light, lying ahead in shadows of blue with the big clouds above them. Riders on the other side of the course go galloping off to follow the race. Part of the crowd trails away to see the horses pass at a distant point in the course.

'Dark Horse wins!' cry men with field-glasses. But it is not certain.

'He's making the running.... He's well away. ... Hullo! Diogenes! He's coming up on the outside.... They're level....'

On they come, neck to neck, the jockeys urging them forward, spending their last ounce of speed; little whips rise and fall above the shining flanks, on they come thudding over the grass, Diogenes and Dark Horse neck to neck, with flecks of white foam at their bridles; then Diogenes seems suddenly to spring forward, a head in front, half a length, a length. ... Diogenes wins!

I go and collect my winnings!

I find myself among a crowd of expert racing-men. They know everything that happens on the Curragh. They know every horse. They know exactly what owner, trainer, and jockey think about them.

'Will your mare win the next race, Bill?'

'No. She's been coughing all the winter.... Have you heard what they say about Green Mantle?'

And so it goes on through the afternoon.

In the evening the racecourse is deserted. The larks are coming down out of the sky and the shadows fall over the great limestone plain.

Opposite page *Cutting a diamond pattern on a vase at the world famous Waterford glass works*

Above left *Turf-cutting, Co. Wicklow*

Above right *Tympanum over the north door of Cormac's Chapel, St Patrick's Rock, Tipperary*

Upper Lake, Glendalough

The charm of Ireland is partly due to the delicious slowness of life. Ireland is a Catholic country, and you feel as in most Catholic countries, but notably in Spain, that the material world is rendered unreal and rather childish because it is overshadowed by the spiritual. The church which abhors secret societies spreads nevertheless through any Catholic country the atmosphere of a secret society; its people belong to something powerful and important which rules their conduct.

Shopkeepers do not seem to be real shopkeepers but to be pretending to be shopkeepers, just as men wheeling barrows along a road appear not to be wheeling them in order to earn money but because they gain some obscure satisfaction in the act. The religion of America, which is conquering England, has of course no foothold in Ireland. This is the belief in the sanctity of production. It must be almost impossible for a Catholic to believe, as many an American manufacturer does, that in producing a new kind of toothpaste or safety razor he is conferring a real benefit on the human race. This inability to believe in the spiritual glory of work gives to Ireland a gentle detachment, and necessarily reflects attention on human personalities.

In England, and in all countries where material things are important, we think of a man first as a grocer, an undertaker, a sanitary inspector, and secondly as a fellow human being. It is almost with a shock that we realize on Sunday afternoons that policemen have plain clothes and children. In Ireland it is different. A customs officer is Mr Casey first and a customs officer a long way after!

If an Irishman wants to accumulate real wealth he must go out of Ireland and shake himself free from an almost oriental detachment. It is this detachment from things that go-ahead nations consider vital, which explains why to some people the Irish never appear serious. Their mental attitude to life is infuriating to the materialist. He calls it laziness. But the Irish are not lazy; they are casual, indolent, and metaphysical. There is a half-sad, half-humorous subjectiveness about Irish life which gives to the country a pensive detachment.

The curse of industrial nations is the cruel and cynical subjection of man to machines. Ireland may be poor, but at least her flesh and blood are not humiliated by that tyranny of mechanical things which is inseparable from the production of modern wealth.

One result of Ireland's casual attitude to work is that the country is a place of amusing makeshifts. Objects long past their normal span are pressed into some service for which their inventors never intended them. An old front door will stop a gap in a hedge, bits of string will hold together some antique motor which in some incredible way continues to work; nothing is ever too old or useless to be thrown away. Mechanical inefficiency which is a shame and a disgrace in the modern world is to an Irishman often merely a thoroughly good joke. But, like the child he is in parts, the Irishman will often pretend that a machine is efficient when it is hopelessly defunct.

Blarney Castle

Kilkenny Cathedral is one of the finest churches in Ireland. It is full of Plantagenet knights lying in full armour holding their swords and gazing upward into eternity. There is an ancient stone seat in which the verger persuades you to sit and wish. Ireland seems more full of wishing-stones and wells than any other part of the earth.

The castle of Kilkenny, which is as feudal-looking as any castle I know, contains many fine pictures and the signature of every English king since Henry II.

It was in Kilkenny that a Parliament was summoned by the viceroy, Lionel, Duke of Clarence, in 1367, when one of the landmarks of Irish history – the Statute of Kilkenny – was directed not only at the native Irish but also at those members of the English colony who had 'gone native', and were known as 'the degenerate English'. The object of the Act was to separate the two races: 'the Irish enemies', as they were called throughout the Act, and the 'degenerate English'. As not one Englishman in twenty thousand could probably give an account of this Act it is worthwhile to outline some of its main points:

Alliance with the Irish by marriage, fosterage (the Irish custom of educating children in the families of another member of the tribe) and gossipred (a baptismal responsibility similar to acting as a godfather) were forbidden as high treason and were to be punished with death.

Above left *The Butler Tomb, St Canice's Cathedral, Kilkenny*

Above right *The National Stud, Tully, Co. Kildare*

Opposite *The south side of Cormac's Chapel*

Any Englishman by birth or blood who took an Irish name, spoke the Irish tongue, wore the Irish dress, or adopted any Irish custom should forfeit his estates.

No Englishman was to allow the Irish to graze cattle on his land, to grant livings to Irish clergy, or to entertain the Irish bards, pipers or story-tellers.

The necessity for such legislation – which was insisted on 137 years later by Poyning's Law – proves how rapidly a nation was forming in Ireland after the invasion. The fusion of Anglo-Norman and Irish, had it been encouraged instead of suppressed, might have altered the course of Anglo-Irish history.

The streets of Kilkenny are old-fashioned and rather grim. There are beautiful walks beside the river, town walls, and several fine religious ruins; but these did not claim my attention – I wandered about the streets in the hope of seeing a couple of Kilkenny cats fighting!

Strangely enough, Kilkenny is full of dogs! It is so full of them that cats, if they exist, keep prudently within doors.

'Why,' I asked a native, 'are Kilkenny cats famous as fighters?'

He said he did not know.

I tried another man who proved to be the usual 'stranger' who never knows anything. At length I found an authority:

'That's easy,' he said. 'There are two stories about it. In the old days there were two towns; one was called Irish-town and one English-town. They fought like cats! The other story is that when Cromwell was here his troopers used to tie a rope across a street, tie two cats together by the tails, sling them over the rope, and watch them fight. Now this was thought cruel, even by Cromwell, which may seem a bit strange; and so

The castle and River Suir, Cahir

an order was given out that no soldier was to amuse himself in this way. . . .

'One day a party of troopers were watching a cat-fight, when two officers were seen approaching. There was no time to separate the cats, so they just cut off their tails! They explained to the officers that the cats had fought until nothing was left but their tails!'

'That is, of course, the Irish version?'

'It is.'

I thanked him, and took the road to Tipperary.

I like the town of Cahir (they pronounce it Carc). I like to stand at an upstair window of the excellent, homely hotel and watch the slow life of the wide main street.

There is often nothing in it but a few old people mysteriously congregated with their donkey carts, standing engaged in conversation and earnestly discussing the price of vegetables. It is a curious, watchful street. Although it is often empty it is never asleep. It is wide as a parade ground, and I imagine that anything happening on it is immediately known all over the town.

Irish country towns vary enormously in atmosphere. Some seem drenched in a hopeless shabbiness. It would be impossible to do any work in them. The only thing to do would be to drink and gloom and make excuses to yourself. But a few miles from such towns are others surprisingly different: bright, clean, hopeful, vaguely busy; and Cahir is like that.

Down the wide street comes a herd of cows. Fine horses go by with plaited manes and tails and numbered cards on their flanks. There is a cattle and horse show somewhere near. A sable priest stands at the corner of the street, and

pauses in his conversation to follow the horse-flesh with his eyes; as in fact everyone does. It is all so peaceful and so drenched in the sanity of the eighteenth century.

The warm afternoon sunlight falls over the square. Down the road comes a man leading a great black bull. There is a ring through its nostrils. Its hide shines like polished ebony. It sways under the weight of its fat and muscle, placing its feet on the road as deliberately as an elephant, and as it goes by it turns its head now and then and looks with unconscious fierceness round it.

Cahir Castle is one of the finest buildings of its kind I have seen in Ireland. It lifts its towers above the River Suir beside a pretty bridge. And from its ramparts you look down to a mill dam and a broad sweep of water that reminds me strangely of Stratford-on-Avon. In the opposite direction you can see the exquisite Suir winding through woodland. There is a bright chequer-work of fields rising to hills that lift themselves against the sky in various subtleties of blue.

So deep a hush lay over the plain of Tipperary that I could hear the dogs barking as far away as Rosegreen and Cahir. The setting sun was almost warm over the plain, and not one whisper of wind moved the grass.

Before me, in the centre of the Golden Vale, rose Cashel of the Kings, that mighty rock, lonely as a great ship at sea, lifted above the flat lands as Ely lifts herself above the fenlands of Cambridgeshire. It is strange that one of Ireland's most sacred relics should have been planted by the devil. Every school-child in Tipperary knows that when the devil was flying home (apparently to England) across the plain

of Tipperary, he took a savage bite out of the northern hills in passing, but dropped the rocky mouthful in the centre of the Golden Vale.

It is a fact that, if you look in the right direction towards the Slieve Bloom Mountains, you can see the gap in the remote hills which Cashel, it seems, would exactly fit. They call it the Devil's Bit.

The Angelus bell was ringing in the still evening as I took the steep path to the ancient stronghold of the Kings of Munster.

On top of this high rock, surrounded by a stone wall, is all that is left of a royal city of ancient Ireland. The man who unlocks the gate and admits you to a wide space of hummocky grass and the ruins of palace and churches points to a rough stone on which is an ancient cross.

'That,' he tells you, 'is where St Patrick baptized King Aengus in the olden days.'

In Cashel they still remember the story of the baptism of King Aengus. I like the familiar way people in Ireland talk about the heroes and kings of antiquity. They might just have left them round the bend of a lane. They say that when King Aengus was baptized on the ancient coronation stone of the high kings at Cashel, St Patrick was old and feeble, and in order to support himself he drove the spiked point of his crozier firmly into the earth. When the ceremony was over St Patrick and those who stood round saw blood in the grass. The crozier had transfixed the foot of the king. The saint asked Aengus why he had not cried out in pain, and the king replied that he had heard so much about the sufferings of our Lord that he would have been proud to bear the agony, even had he not considered it part of the ceremony.

More wonderful than the round tower of

Previous page *Lismore Castle above the River Blackwater*

Chancel Arch of St Saviour's Priory, Glendalough

Cashel, more interesting than the vague lines of the ancient palace, more beautiful than the roofless shell of the cathedral is King Cormac's Chapel, the most whimsical, the most strange and the most remarkable little chapel in the British Isles.

If you visit Ireland only to see this astonishing building you will not have crossed the sea in vain. It is the strangest sight to one accustomed to Norman churches in England, built by the Normans – apparently with a chisel in one hand and a drawn sword in the other! Durham Cathedral, which is the greatest Norman Church in England, holds something of Flambard's sternness in its stones. Even small chapels, like St John's in the Tower of London and that practically unknown underground chapel in the Black Keep at Newcastle, are essentially grim. They appear to have been designed by architects who had just composed a fortress. But Cormac's Chapel on Cashel is the only piece of gay Norman architecture I have seen. One might call it Norman architecture with a sense of humour! There is nothing else quite like it in the world.

What is the explanation? It is the only great piece of Norman work in the British Isles not built by Normans. It was built half a century before the Normans invaded Ireland by those much-travelled Irish monks who, in the early days, went out from their monasteries to every part of Europe. These monks tried to copy something which they had admired very much in France, but it worked out with a Celtic difference: they put into this chapel – into its rounded dome – toothed arches, something quite original, which you will find only in the Book of Kells and the Shrine of St Patrick's Bell.

'And do you not see something strange about the chapel?' asked the guide.

I followed his glance, and noticed that it is at a slightly different angle from the nave, symbolizing the drooping of Christ's head on the Cross. This is the earliest declination I remember to have seen.

If I were an Irishman I would haunt Cashel of the Kings, for there, and there alone, is visible a link with the Gaelic Ireland which, subjected to invasion and oppression, has stubbornly survived: the Ireland of the Book of Kells, the Ardagh Chalice, the Cross of Cong and the Tara brooch. All these things prove a rich and imaginative national life which never had the opportunity to develop.

The view from the perilous wall which is on a level with the cone of the round tower is one of the grandest in Ireland. I can compare it only with the view down over the Links of Forth from the height of Stirling Castle. All round is the fat, green country of the Golden Vale: the thin roads crossing running through fields; the farms; the little belts of woodland and, to the southward, hills.

When it grew dark a great yellow moon swung up over Tipperary plain and hung in the sky above Cashel. The dogs were howling far off in distant farms. Little knots of young men idled and talked at the street corners, laughing and joking and speaking English woven on a Gaelic loom. And on the hill I looked up at the ancient ruins of Cashel of the Kings, rising darkly against the stars. It was silent, empty, and locked for the night, and the moon's light was over it, falling down on it like a green rain.

It rode in moonlight over Tipperary like a haunted ship.

The road that runs due south from Cashel,
through Cahir and Clogheen over the mountains to Lismore is one of the most beautiful I
have ever travelled. You have the wide Plain of
Tipperary round you for miles and facing you
are the Knockmealdown Mountains. Just beyond Clogheen the road rises and you mount
quickly into the wild hills. You come to a
hairpin bend, the Devil's Elbow (his other elbow
is in Scotland on the Blairgowrie road to
Braemar!) and, when you can safely do so, stop
and look back.

This is one of the grandest views in the
British Isles. Below you lies the great Plain of
Tipperary with the little white roads criss-
crossing through the greenness of fields and the
darker green of woods. West of Cahir are the
Galtee Mountains and on the east is
Slievenamon. On a good day you can see the
Rock of Cashel rising up from the green plain
twenty miles to the north.

It is difficult to tear yourself away from such a
sight. But the road goes on and up into
mountains, bare and barren and brown; then it
falls to one of the sweetest glens in the world
where a laughing stream runs beside you all the
way to Lismore.

Here on the banks of the broad, slow
Blackwater – a mighty salmon stream – rises the
magnificent Castle of Lismore which is owned
by the Duke of Devonshire – the Warwick
Castle of Ireland. It is not perhaps as fine as
Warwick but the mind immediately connects
them, both majestic, both throned on wooded
rocks, both reflected in water.

The courtyard of this castle is one of its chief
beauties. The view downward from the drawing-
room is terrifying. No wonder that the timid
James II, who spent a night at Lismore during
his flight from the Battle of the Boyne, started

back in horror from it when he looked from one
of the windows.

Lismore is delightful, a clean, reserved and
dignified country town. I was pleased to find two
kilted pipers, wearing Black Watch tartan,
playing in the streets. When I hailed them as
Scotsmen they answered me in the accents of
Cork!

'It's Irish we are entirely,' they said. 'Would
ye care to subscribe some little thing, now, to
the pipe band of Cark?'

It was a hot, sunny day. The wheels of a donkey
cart had parted company in the main street of
Cork. The sun poured down on a laughing,
animated crowd that would not have seemed
out of place in Seville.

I know no other country which sees such
humour in the, at times, almost evil intracta-
bility of inanimate objects. In England a
breakdown in the road is a shameful spectacle.
It reflects discredit on the person involved. It is
inefficient. The debris is at once rushed to the
side and the business of life sweeps on. In
England a breakdown is a matter for anger; in
Ireland for laughter. This argues a different
philosophy of life. Perhaps only nations with a
profound spiritual attitude to life can laugh at
the occasional failure of material affairs. Or
perhaps that is the reflection of a mind becoming tuned-in to the subtlety of Ireland; for no
man can live for even a week in Ireland, as in
Spain, without looking for a religious explanation to any peculiarity.

The old man to whom this disaster had
happened in the main street of Cork was
apparently a familiar character. The crowd
evidently knew him well. He was so much of an
artist that when he saw that his trouble was

causing amusement he could not deny himself the pleasure of an audience. He therefore determined to make the most of his misfortunes. He addressed himself in the most droll and idiotic way to the placid donkey, conscious perhaps that his display of emotion heightened the humour of the beast's calm and uncomprehending conduct in a situation with which it had been so intimately concerned. He bewailed the accident with ludicrous lamentations and gave a performance which, taken together with the donkey's stupid complacence would have been worth thirty pounds a week to him could he have repeated it twice a night on the English music-hall stage.

Cork was the most foreign city I had seen in Ireland – foreign not in appearance but in atmosphere. One was surprised to hear the crowds talking a high-pitched English. I felt that on a summer's day Cork should be full of vivid striped umbrellas, beneath which the visitor might sit in the shade and sip grenadine.

It was in 1920 that at the height of the madness of the 'Trouble' half Cork was burnt down. I felt sorry that Cork had not taken advantage of this disaster to rebuild its streets in a fashion more in keeping with the distinctive character of its people.

Cork is the capital of Munster: if anything should happen to Dublin it would be, obviously, the capital of the Free State. It is built on an island in the centre of the River Lee. A man, who should have known better, told me that it gets its name because it floats like a cork on the water. Cork, however, is derived from an Irish word meaning marsh.

There is a legend in Ireland to the effect that a Cork man can make a fortune where any other man would be applying for outdoor relief. It is certainly true that the people of Cork are different from the people in other parts of Ireland. They have a tradition as aristocratic as that of Dublin. They are clannish. For centuries they intermarried within their own walls, so that a family feeling exists between all men of Cork, which explains why when a Cork man takes over a business, say in Dublin, other men of Cork appear as if by magic in the firm.

Brilliant conversation began in Cork during the eighteenth century, and it is still going on. It is carried on in a quick, high-pitched, musical Welsh accent. (Or have the Welsh a Cork accent?)

They stay up so late in Cork making epigrams that the shops do not open until 9.30 to 10 a.m. There are certain things in all historic cities which tourists and no other people do. They are generally of a nature to confirm local inhabitants in a belief that all tourists are half-witted. In Cork you are supposed to kiss the Blarney Stone and to hear the bells of Shandon.

Kissing the Blarney Stone is a difficult and not too pleasant act. It is hard to discover why generations of travellers have endured it, and still more difficult to know why that particular stone, 150 feet above the ground level, achieved its world-wide fame.

The dictionary says that blarney is 'to talk over, or beguile by wheedling speech; flatter; humbug with agreeable talk'. When the lift-boy in the hotel heard that I had kissed the Blarney Stone he said, with a grin:

'Och, sir, and now all the young ladies'll be afther ye. . . .'

This represents the cynical local tradition that the Blarney Stone imparts the power of such picturesque deception to the tongue of a man that no woman can resist him. I cannot believe this. As a humble student of human beings I have observed that women, while they on occasions enjoy lies enormously and even at times demand them, can see them sticking up out of man's conversation like rocks in a sea. Still, the influence of blarney on romance is a fruitful and unexplored subject.

I have formed no ideas on it!

The village of Blarney lies five miles to the north-west of Cork.

In the middle of a pretty wood rise the ruins of Blarney Castle, with rooks cawing round it, moss growing over it, and damp green slime in its dungeons. It is the third castle built on that site. The first was a wooden fortress erected in remote times by Dermot McCarthy, King of South Munster; the second was built about A.D. 1200, and the present tattered shell was constructed in the reign of Queen Elizabeth. It was the strongest castle in that part of Ireland. In it lived the younger branch of the princely McCarthys, lords of Muskerry, barons of Blarney, and earls of Clancarthy.

The word 'blarney' entered the language, so they say, when Dermot McCarthy was required to surrender the fortress to Queen Elizabeth as a proof of his loyalty. He said that he would be delighted to do so, but – something always happened at the last moment to prevent the surrender! His excuses became so frequent and were so plausible that the Lord President, Sir George Carew, who was demanding the castle in the name of the Queen, became a joke at Court.

Queen Elizabeth (probably) said, when these excuses were repeated to her: 'Odds bodikins, more Blarney talk!'

In any event the term 'blarney' invaded the English language, meaning plausible wheedling.

The first question you ask when you enter Blarney Castle is, 'Where's the Blarney Stone?'

A caretaker points skywards to the turret of the donjon. You see, 150 feet from the earth, and on the outside of the walls, a large brown stone. Your enthusiasm begins to wane! You go round and round a spiral staircase and emerge on the turret.

In the old days people who kissed the Blarney Stone were hung by the heels over the edge of the parapet. One day a pilgrim broke from the grasp of his friends, and went hurtling into space, and since that time the Blarney Stone has been approached by a different method.

You sit down with your back to a sheer drop of 150 feet. Your guide then sits on your legs, holds your feet, and tells you to lie back over the drop and grasp two iron hand-rails. You are then lying flat on your back with half your body ready for eternity. By wriggling down (and closing your eyes to shut out the distant inverted landscape) you bring yourself to kiss the base of the stone. You then lever yourself up from the abyss, shout: 'Are you sure you've got me?' sit up and say, 'Well; I did it!'

How did this custom originate?

No one knows. It is the kind of thing a caretaker with a sound knowledge of psychology might invent in a moment of inspiration. Kissing the Blarney Stone was unknown in the eighteenth century.

Since then, I discover, there have been many Blarney Stones. There is, in fact, a dispute on the position of the original rock of Blarney. Some say that it is twenty feet from the top of the tower at its southern angle, and bears the inscription, 'Cormac McCarthy fortis mi fieri fecit. A.D. 1446.' Others say that it bears a shamrock in relief and is in a position known to few people. It is discouraging to learn this after you have endured the ordeal!

74

3
KERRY

Kerry is a magic corner of Ireland. Just as in the Isle of Skye you expect something terrible to rise in the dusk from any boulder, so in Kerry you expect something weird to stand up at any moment beside you on the hills. One day alone in Kerry, away from the roads on mountains that go down sharply to the sea, and you understand why in lonely places the Irish believe in fairies and things not of this earth.

The Kerry villages are poor and small and, many of them, dirty. In small towns there is no apparent social life. There are no book shops. There are no village institutes; no libraries. There seems to be no public spirit. There are days when a kind of death seems to come to these towns. They might be infected with a plague. The streets are empty. The shopkeepers stand listlessly in their small and often redundant stores. A few loungers lurk at corners holding switches cut from a hedge and looking as if they had lost a herd of cows. The listlessness of these stagnating townships is sometimes almost terrible. But some towns of a size which in England might give a lean living to three solicitors have a sort of lawyers' quarter – a little Temple whose brass plates are like a shining testimony to the pugnacity of the Irish farmer. A law case brings life into them!

Now and again a man comes out of a shop and slowly crosses the empty main street. You are told that he is the local Midas – Mr Maloney who has twenty thousand pounds in the bank. It is, apparently, always 'in the bank'! Mr Maloney would never think of investing it. He would also never dream of doing anything to enliven or improve life in the town. At regular intervals the chapel bell rings.

In many remote Scottish towns and villages

Evening at the Lower Lake, Killarney

Previous page *A typical Kerry cottage in Glencar*

Near Moll's Gap

there is always a more or less talkative elderly
man who will, when given a glass of whisky, tell
you how he *almost* invented something that
would have made his fortune, only, alas, just as
he was getting it right someone else got in
ahead and reaped the benefit! In remote Irish
towns his prototype is a genealogist. He will
over a glass of porter tell you all about the local
ancestors. He stands in Mike Finnigan's drink-
shop brooding about parentage. He knows
everything about everybody.

'– D'ye see that man now?' he will ask, half
turning from the saloon counter and pointing
with his pipe to indicate a man in the street,
'That's Paddy Milligan, the Sheep Stealer!'

'What?' you ask, surprised. 'Does he steal
sheep?'

A grim, condemnatory look will come into the
man's face and he will tell you solemnly:

'Shure his grandfather was *hanged* for sheep
stealing!'

His grandfather! You find it difficult not to
laugh! Just because generations ago a man's
forbears were barbarously hanged for theft his
descendant is condemned to walk about modern
Ireland in a sort of reflected villainy! I wonder
how much of Ireland's sorrow has been caused
by this trick of looking backwards instead of
forwards, in nursing old grievances, in putting
salt on old wounds. The patriot will say,
perhaps, that Ireland never had anything to
look forward to and was therefore forced to look
backwards. Is that just? Surely this habit of
living in the past is a common Gaelic habit of
mind. The Highlanders of Scotland possess it in
a marked degree. It always accompanies a
passion for genealogy.

I would go day after day to read among the ruins of the big house beside the road. It was quiet and mysterious. The weeds had made a riot of the garden, but roses still flowered. All I knew about the big house was that at some time during the 'Trouble' the owners were turned out and the place fired by the Irregulars. There was not far from the house, in a shrubbery, the remains of an ancient wall and tower, all that was left of a fortress. The place had evidently been occupied for centuries.

The dead house began to fascinate me. I would prowl about in the ruins looking at the blackened walls and the faded wall-paper, the places where pictures had hung, the staring windows, doors which led nowhere, stairs that ended in mid-air; and I would wonder what kind of people lived there and what they had done to deserve this.

I asked questions about it and bit by bit pieced together its history; and in the story of that piece of land was also the history of Ireland.

When in the year A.D. 1171 Henry II became Ireland's first absentee landlord, he left behind him a Norman baron (Welsh on his mother's side, like so many of the original invaders) in possession of this estate. The six-foot-thick boundary wall in the shrubbery is all that remains of the castle built by this settler.

This Norman family settled down and developed along that line of least resistance which had it not violently conflicted with the ideas of England's rulers might have solved the 'Irish Question' centuries ago. In the course of a few generations this family became, to all appearances, Irish. It spoke Irish, intermarried with Irish families, observed the Brehon Law, adopted the Irish system of fosterage, and changed its name to – say – MacFerris. Such union between the English and the Irish was hateful to Westminster. Such families were known as the 'degenerate English'. The Statute of Kilkenny was launched against them in 1367. The MacFerris family, however, managed to weather the storms of three centuries, until a bright light of burning in the sky announced the arrival of Cromwell on his war of extermination. Then the MacFerris family was driven into the hills. That was in the year A.D. 1653.

The new owner of this estate was one of Cromwell's Puritan followers, a soldier named – say – Buckley. He took the MacFerris demesne, built himself a suitable house, and established himself on the land. He weathered the Stuart storms as successfully as his predecessor had weathered those of Plantagenet times.

The Georgian age found these Buckleys no longer humble ex-servicemen of Cromwell's but distinguished country gentlemen with Gainsboroughs and Romneys on their walls, good wine in the cellar, and a stable full of noble horses. The house of their ancestors had made way for an austere square mansion with a portico upheld by Corinthian columns. They were, by comparison with others, good landlords and well liked. They disappeared for long periods into England, where their rents were sent to them. Here the process of Irishing which had penalized the Plantagenet settlers was a kind of social charm. The Buckleys when in England were considered to be delightfully Irish. They were expected to do and say funny things and to be generally a bit mad. But they could not speak Gaelic and they were staunch Protestants. (When they returned to Ireland their tenants thought of them as English.)

They sent sons into the Army and the Church. A Buckley distinguished himself in the Crimea. Another became an English Bishop. In Victoria's reign – so glorious and well-fed for

England, so miserable and starved for Ireland – the Buckleys heard the first faint rumble of rebellion, but they rode to hounds right through it. They served in the South African War, and a Buckley commanded an English yeomanry regiment during the war with Germany.

This was the Colonel Buckley who had come over to see his agent in 1922. He discovered that the warning rumble of Fenianism through which his great-grandfather and his grandfather had hunted now swept with the force of a gale through Ireland. The young men of his estate seemed to belong to a secret society. He saw strange slogans chalked up on the walls. His tenants had the appearance of spies. One night, he was sitting at dinner in the big Georgian room, congratulating himself, perhaps, that the good deeds of his ancestors had preserved his Irish fortunes, when there was a tramp of feet as a band of Irregulars walked in, tough young men with caps pulled over their eyes. He had time to notice among them the sons of one or two of his tenants.

'You've got your rosary?' one began from force of habit; then, remembering that the Colonel was a Protestant he smiled grimly and said: 'Come on now to the top of the hill.'

The Buckleys, like most of the unfortunate Anglo-Irish, may at times have been stupid but they were never cowardly. The Colonel, knowing at once that he was about to be murdered, and knowing too that argument was pointless, asked to be allowed to find a hat. They marched him to the top of his own hill in the dark. Here a huge young man stood over him.

'Who does that demesne belong to, Colonel Buckley?' he asked.

'It belongs to me,' said the Colonel.

'Oh; it does?' replied the young man with

Stock being offered for sale at the Killarney Animal Fair is not penned but usually tethered or simply herded into a quiet corner by the farmer

Windy Gap, Killarney

deep irony. 'Well, now, take a good look at me while you can! That demesne belonged to me before you came over with Cromwell. My name's MacFerris! Now down with ye on your knees. . . .'

But the Colonel was not shot. At the last moment the men, becoming alarmed by a scouting-party of Free State troops, fled, leaving the middle-aged Anglo-Irishman kneeling on the grass without the slightest idea that Cromwellian had met Plantagenet. As the Colonel rose he looked down and saw that his house was on fire. He then and there swore never to set foot on Irish soil; and he kept his vow. He retired to an English cathedral city.

So I go day after day to read among the ruins of the house beside the road. There is something as inevitable as Greek tragedy in the thought of a MacFerris, probably a farm-labourer, swooping down with the indignation of centuries behind him to snatch a brief vengeance at the pistol's point. If this long memory is not nationalism what is it?

There is not a great estate in Ireland owned by one of Cromwell's settlers which had not always had a ghostly other owner in the memory of the common people. He may be only a legend or he may be somebody living 'up in the hills'; but he is not forgotten.

It all proves that in Ireland there is no ancient history: all history is contemporary. It also suggests a number of other things.

It is odd that Ireland should have the reputation of a gay and rollicking country. I suppose the hard-drinking, hard-riding Anglo-Irish of the Georgian age are responsible for this legend.

As the road goes on into Kerry I come across stretches of country from which melancholy seems to ooze from the hard soil. There is a sadness and a disillusion in the air. The very rain weeps rather than falls over the land and the wind is a sigh. I compare such places with happy countrysides: the fat orchard lands of Herefordshire; Kent with the hops ripening in tall battalions; the vineyards of Burgundy; the silver plain round Avignon; the saintly country about Siena; the plump cloudy dairy-lands of Holland.

There can be nothing in the world like the sadness of some parts of Ireland. The rain might be the tears of exiles; the wind might be the crying of those forced to die in foreign lands. It is an atmosphere which speaks of centuries of hunger, eviction, and emigration.

Next page, left *Gap of Dunloe, Killarney*

Next page, right *Garinish Island Gardens, Glengarriff*

Loading nets into a fishing boat at Dingle Harbour

Ireland is as moody as its people. Just as an Irishman will follow a mood of laughter with one almost of tears, so this country changes in a few miles from a cheerful, quiet, knowing region to a dreary, sorrowful, neglected area of depression which has, so far as I know, never been described in fiction. If some writer with E. Somerville's gift of humour and John Galsworthy's gift of pity had in some way combined these two atmospheric extremes we might have had a true novel of Ireland. It seems to me that the pictures of Irish life are desperately incomplete. Behind all the laughter, the horse-coping, the steeplechasing, the drinking, the intrigue is a character who never appears, but one who has proved himself the most important in modern Irish history: the sullen countryman with a pitchfork. He stands behind a stone wall watching the hunt go by, a member of an inferior race but, in his own imagination, the descendant of saints and kings.

And in these sad parts of Ireland it seems that his long memory has filled the air with a hard resentment, and perhaps the pathos has been put into it by women who have seen their children go hungry to bed. . . .

This may be fantastic. Ireland encourages fantastic thought. Any true book on Ireland must be full of contradictions and thoughts that may be only half true.

I went on by the lovely coast road round Bantry Bay and came to rest in a heavenly place called Glengariff.

It is difficult to believe in London. Is it possible that crowds at this moment are moving along Piccadilly, that a line of traffic halts on Ludgate Hill, that men are seriously worried

The harbour, Glengarriff

Next page *The side stalls do a brisk trade at the Killarney Animal Fair*

about catching a train to Manchester or Bradford? In Glengariff such thoughts are grotesque. Here nothing has happened since the police barracks were burned down in the 'Trouble'. There is nothing else to burn down, so one can venture to say that nothing is likely to happen here again. . . .

Old Mick and I potter about on a frail little boat over the creeks and baylets as men might potter round a garden, nosing our way over still waters, round tiny islands, listening to the silence – silence so deep that the splash of a careless oar is like a cough in church.

Small things here are enormously important. I give my whole attention – and so does Old Mick – to the flight of gulls and to the seals which bob about in the sea round the outer islands. The gannets are interesting. They cruise high overhead, slowly, deliberately, then, having spotted a fish, they just drop through the air beak first like white darts and cleave the sea with the splash of a small calibre shell. They remain under water for some time and reappear in an unexpected direction looking satisfied.

Mick says they often do a six-foot dive in pursuit of their prey. He combines a rare love of natural beauty with the countryman's carelessness for animal life. He wants to show me how easy it is to kill gannets. All you have to do is to place a fish on the gunwale of the boat. The gannets dive to it and break their necks; which is stupid of them. Mick cannot understand why I threaten to beat him about his venerable head with an oar if he attempts to do this!

There are guillemots, like little penguins, who sit up in the sea and wave their tiny wings; there are kittiwakes, there are sea-parrots with red beaks, oyster-catchers, and wild geese. Occasionally a blue heron lifts himself from the

93

rushes and flaps his way slowly to a new island.

In still little bays the water is the colour of pale jade. The bed of the sea is studded with stones like jewels and shell-fish of queer and attractive design.

Old Mick tells me that he has brought up a family of twelve children on potatoes, buttermilk, fish, and an occasional egg. They are healthy children, and the three in America are doing well.

'They're in the next village,' says Old Mick, waggishly, nodding his head towards the Atlantic.

He has never been to Dublin. The City of Cork has seen him once or twice. London is to him a mere abstraction, as remote as Moscow. America, however, is a reality. His ragged pockets are stuffed with American newspaper cuttings sent home by the exiles. He knows all about New York.

'Aye, it's a hard life entirely,' says Old Mick. 'It's a very divil of a life when young children are growing, but you can't starve with the sea full of fish and the rocks covered with mussels as big as duck eggs; and you can't freeze with turf in the bog. . . . I'm thinking there's some in the cities have a harder time, and they with money in a bank. . . .'

Och, sure now, he wouldn't change places with the king of England!

We were cruising one morning near the islands which lie like ships at anchor in the bay. All round us were mountains washed in every unlikely tint of blue, from the grey blue of a Colmar grape to the deep blue of the violet. The woods marched down to the water's edge, and there was no sign of man on land or sea. This is the Riviera of Ireland!

'That's the view Mr Bernard Shaw thinks the finest view in all the countries of the earth,' said

The Skelligs

Next page *Evening on the Lower Lake, Killarney*
Inset *Ross Castle, Killarney*

Old Mick suddenly and surprisingly.

'And who is Mr Bernard Shaw?' I asked him.

'Och, sure, he's a nice quiet man with a beard on him. And he's written a lot of his pomes on the island there. Pomes just spring from um as he's walking round Garinish Island. . . . He comes from London, but they do say he's a Dublin man. . . .'

I tried to reconcile the restless personality of G.B.S. – the famous poet! – with the serenity of Garinish Island, which we approached over a placid sea. When we rounded the point we saw a boat-house and a steam-launch on the beach. We disembarked under the scrutiny of an ancient man like a leprechaun, who, instead of hopping away into the bushes, advanced and told us that the garden gate was open.

Garinish Island is part of the magic of Glengariff. It has no right to be there! It is an affront to one's sense of probability! Such things happen only in fairy-tales.

Here, facing the Atlantic Ocean, marooned in the wildest and most primitive portion of Southern Ireland, is a perfect Italian garden with pergolas, rock gardens, a marble pond full of gold-fish, Roman statues on marble pedestals, sombre, cone-shaped cypress trees, and every conceivable flower and flowering shrubs. It might have been blown over from the hills round Florence on the wings of some magic gale.

The solitude is deathlike. There is no sound but the cries of wild birds and the bleating of black-faced sheep. There is no movement but the clouds which steam gently over the crests of the mountains. The road to Killarney winds round and up through a gorge as destitute of life as the Valley of the Dead in Egypt.

When I turned a corner I saw approaching slowly over the mountain path a coffin lying in a motor-car. Behind were three cars full of women with white, tear-stained faces. A mourner ran beside the coffin tightening the ropes that held it in position. This funeral might have been a vision called up by the grim spirit of the hills.

So I went on for twenty miles into a wilder solitude, watching the cloud-shadows racing down the hillsides, watching the clouds dip down into the valleys to float suspended there, watching the flight of some wild bird as it launched itself into space. This pass is drenched in the uncanny mystery of all high places; over it is the watchful hush of hills and sky. Then – Windy Gap!

Is there a greater surprise in the British Isles? With a suddenness that takes the breath away you are faced by one of the grandest views in Europe! There is no warning. You emerge from the wilderness as suddenly as a man leaving a dark tunnel comes into the light of day. You do not expect it! You can hardly believe it! Behind you the abomination of desolation; below you an earthly paradise – the three blue Lakes of Killarney.

I rested on a stone wall and stayed in a kind of dream, gazing down at the amazing bird's-eye view of the lakes, the blue mountains, and the green woods. It was a warm, sunny day. The lakes were the colour of the sky and as still as glass. A boat smaller than a leaf moved slowly over the water, and I could see men pulling at a salmon net.

Every graciousness and softness that nature has denied the mountains have been poured out into the rich valley of Killarney. It is almost too good to be true; almost too opulent to be quite credible. You feel, as you look down on it, that it might at any moment dissolve into mist, leaving you in the stern reality of the hills. . . .

A man rested his horse and came over to the stone wall. He pointed out the tall crests of Macgillicuddy's Reeks; and, turning to the left, indicated the mountain of Mangerton, an extinct volcano of which the crater is a lake so deep that its water looks like black ink. The wildest storm never ruffles the Devil's Punch Bowl; the hottest summer day never varies its icy temperature. They say that it is 700 feet deep; and they believe that if a childless woman who longs for a child climbs Mangerton and drinks the icy water of this lake she will gain her wish.

'It's been proved time and again!' said the man, giving me the names of two English peers who, said he, owe their existence to the magic of Mangerton!

I suggested that it must be a wonderful thing to live under the influence of such scenery. He turned his back on the lakes and, gazing over the wild hills, said that strange people lived in the 'black valley'. He told me of queer, hidden places which no man really knows, and of a shy, hostile race, different from ordinary Kerry folk, who live by poaching and mix only with their own kind.

He went his way, and I dipped down into the almost tropical luxuriance of Killarney.

In the early morning the lakes are covered with a white mist which curls over them in a thousand strange, suggestive shapes. This is the time when you can see the O'Donoghue of the Glens riding over the water on his white horse.

When the sun is strong the hills become blue and purple and mauve. You can spend days in the woods and thickets marvelling at the incredible richness of the soil. (I believe they could grow date palms in Killarney!) There is a touch of jungle vegetation about it. Tall palm trees lift their spiky heads against the blue sky. Kerry is warmer in winter than any other part of the British Isles. In the month of February, I am told, spring is already in Killarney moving through the hedge and woodland, the gorse is in

Beehive stone chamber used as a pigsty near Beenacouma on Slea Head, near Dingle

full bloom, the chestnut buds are unfolding.

In summer Killarney is a botanist's paradise. Here grow cedars of Lebanon, arbutus, wild fuchsia, the Mediterranean strawberry tree, which is unknown elsewhere in the British Isles, the scented orchid, which grows along the Mediterranean coast and in Asia Minor, the great butterwort, which is a native of Spain, the 'blue-eyed grass', which you will see only in Canada.

The boatmen and the jarveys of Killarney are expert at feeling your pulse. They have a genius for telling you what you expect them to tell you! They sum you up in ten seconds. A silent Scotsman who has been fishing at Killarney for three years assured me that he had the services of the ideal guide. He had barely spoken one word a year! (I learned afterwards that the guide is famous as the most garrulous old man in Kerry!)

'Are there any leprechauns in Killarney?' I asked a jarvey.

'Leprechauns?' he said, taking a good look at me. 'Why, this is the most terrible place in all Ireland for them! You could not stir a foot in the old days for them. . . .'

Then he told me a story about a wicked land agent and a hunchback farmer. (The land agent is always the villain in Irish fairy-tales!) The leprechauns, in order to reward the hunchback farmer for refusing to level the fort in which they lived, moved his hump to the land agent!

The sun sinks behind the mountains, mists like grey veils lie in the hollow of the hills, the lake water is silver white, the chill wind of evening blows through the ruined garden, and the first star burns over the entrancing loveliness of Killarney.

There was once a Frenchman, I am told, who said that Ireland was the jewel of the West, that Kerry was the jewel of Ireland, that Killarney was the jewel of Kerry, and that the little uninhabited Isle of Innisfallen was the jewel of Killarney. I have nothing to add to this.

In the centre of the Lower Lake is this enchanted island. I wandered there for two days, never meeting a living soul, listening to the lapping of lake water and the wind in the trees.

Half-hidden by shrubs is the grey ghost of Innisfallen Abbey, where in the old days Brian Boru was educated. This abbey, like the churches of Glendalough, Cormac's Chapel on the Rock of Cashel, and the ruins on the Skellig Rocks, goes back to the days of the saints. It is one of the many homes of early Christianity in the West, and in it Christ was worshipped when England lay storm-tossed in those centuries of paganism which followed the end of the Roman occupation.

I would like to see the shrubs uprooted from it. The ivy should be pulled from its walls. It seems to me to demand this as surely as Cormac's Chapel, the most magnificent piece of architecture in Ireland and the finest example of Romanesque work in the British Isles, demands protection from the deadly green damp that will some day ruin it.

I know of no more perfect place than Innisfallen in which to spend a summer day. It is a country in miniature: it has its hills and valleys, its little green pasture-lands, its dark woods, its creeks and its bays. There is a holy peace over it; and a man, parting the thick bushes, comes on the old grey ruin almost fearfully, thinking as he stands before the altar whose cloth is a green moss that if a saint wished to show himself to men this is the place where he might shine a moment, his sandals deep in summer flowers.

LIMERICK TO CONNEMARA

I left Killarney in a mist that developed into rain along the road to Tralee. How it can rain in Ireland! With what exaggerated enthusiasm it falls in straight sheets hour after hour. I passed through drenched villages and towns that stood helpless in the downpour, the rain dripping from their roofs, splashing upward from the roads, gurgling in the gutters, blowing round corners; and there was hardly a soul to be seen but some daring person with a sack over his shoulders making a run for it from door to door. Tralee, Listowel, Athea and Rathkeale, all looked much the same, equally grey, deserted and abandoned to the rain.

Suddenly it grew thinner and ceased; and I came, by one of those unbelievable transitions not uncommon in Ireland, into an improbable place called Adare. I think Adare is the happiest-looking village in Ireland. It looks cosy, comfortable, prosperous, its wide road is flanked by model houses, and there are even flowers in the gardens.

Everything about Adare spoke of some presiding genius. Someone loved the place, spent money on it and made the best of it and enjoyed doing it. I learnt that behind the long wall beside the tall trees against the road was the seat of the Earls of Dunraven, and the Earls of Dunraven, I was told, had created Adare.

I was much tempted to spend the night in the charming hotel which bears their name, but I tore myself away from this lucky village and splashed on in the direction of Limerick. It is a big, sprawling city that, like Edinburgh, re-created itself during the eighteenth century. Just as Edinburgh marched down from the rock and built that Georgian district whose backbone is Prince's Street, so Limerick at much the same time built a

Near Kilkeiran, Co. Galway

rectangular district called Newton Pery, after Mr Sexton Pery who became Lord Glentworth, a title now merged in that of the Earl of Limerick. This new town of Mr Pery's is modern Limerick; but Old Limerick still exists in English Town and Irish Town, those inevitable and eloquent components of Anglo-Irish civic life, which correspond to the Canongate of Edinburgh. Those ancient districts face one another over a narrow piece of water. English Town had the best of it. It is built on an island and had a good castle to defend it; Irish Town had none of these advantages although later on in history the walls of Limerick enclosed it.

The memory of Limerick that I, and I suppose everyone, takes away is that of a fine bridge over the Shannon which at this point is a wide and splendid river. At one end of this bridge rise the massive rounded towers of an ancient castle; at the other end is one of the sights of Ireland: a big, rough boulder now much chipped by souvenir hunters which stands mounted on a plinth. This is the famous 'Treaty Stone'.

Ireland's heroes are unknown in the wide sense of the word to all except those of Irish blood. How many Englishmen could give an account of Red Hugh O'Donnell, Sarsfield, Lord Edward Fitzgerald, Robert Emmet or Daniel O'Connell; yet where is the Englishman to whom Wallace, Bruce, John Knox, Mary Stuart, Montrose and Prince Charles Edward are not as familiar as the heroes of his own country?

Scotland has flung the veil of romance over her history. She has made her national story admired and beloved all over the world; but Ireland has been too busy making heroes to achieve that mood of detachment in which great historical romances are written. But the time will come.

Ireland's heroes are magnificent. They stand out against the sombre background of their times with the elemental splendour of all who, defying fearful odds, are willing to pay for defiance with their lives.

When a man stands at the Treaty Stone of Limerick he remembers a hero whom any nation would be proud to honour: Patrick Sarsfield.

It is the first of July 1690.

A horseman is riding to Dublin through the summer night. He makes for the house of Lord Tyrconnel, the Lord Lieutenant of Ireland. Those who see him know that the Jacobite cause is lost. He is that futile and unfortunate man, King James II. 'Our good king James is an excellent and worthy man,' once said the Duchess of Orleans, 'but the most foolish person I have ever encountered. Piety has made him positively stupid.'

This night he has much to occupy him. He is flying for his life. He tells Lady Tyrconnel how he was beaten by his son-in-law, William III, at Boyne Water. He tells her bitterly that his Irish army ran away.

'But,' replies her ladyship, 'your majesty won the race.'

The next day he rides to Kinsale where a French man-o'-war takes him and his ruined hopes into exile.

But the struggle continues. It is really three struggles wrapped up as one. It is the struggle of a Stuart king to regain the throne of his fathers. It is the struggle of Britain and her Protestant allies to oppose the ascendancy in Europe of Catholic France. It is the struggle of the Protestant Anglo-Scots and the Catholic Irish for the leadership of Ireland.

The Irish forces mass on the west coast.

Tyrconnel, who was as incompetent as James, follows his master to France and the commander of the Jacobite force is Patrick Sarsfield. He is an Anglo-Irishman, a brooding, melancholy, modest man, a great patriot and fearless. He had learnt his soldiering as an officer in the English army. He decides to put Limerick in a condition to stand a siege. He has with him 20,000 foot and 4,500 horse.

The garrison work day and night to strengthen the walls of the city, to mount cannon and to store munitions, and hardly have they done so before King William and his army arrive and seize all passages over the Shannon north of the city. One man from the royalist army finds his way into Limerick and seeks out Sarsfield. He is a Huguenot deserter. He tells Sarsfield that King William has summoned a siege train from Dublin that is already on its way with quantities of gunpowder, cannon and pontoons.

Sarsfield determines on the gallant and reckless venture of intercepting and destroying the convoy.

That night while Limerick is snatching its uneasy sleep, and as the sentinels watch the camp fires of the enemy, five hundred horsemen steal out of the beleaguered city on the stroke of midnight. Patrick Sarsfield leads them and with him is a daring soldier, Galloping O'Hogan, a man who knows every inch of the countryside.

They ride cautiously through the darkness, moving to the north, taking a wide sweep to avoid the enemy outposts, and they cross the Shannon at Killaloe. They dare not be seen in daylight. In the few hours of darkness left to them they gain the glens of Keeper Hill. There they hide all that day while a few scouts are sent out to report the route of the convoy.

When night falls again the five hundred horsemen saddle and mount, taking the road to

Ballyneety, only seventeen miles from Limerick, where the convoy has halted for the night. As they go through the darkness Sarsfield learns with grim enjoyment that the enemy have chosen his own name as the night's pass-word!

As they approach the camp a sentry challenges:

'Halt! Give the pass-word.'

'Sarsfield!' replies Sarsfield.

'All's well. Pass on!'

The five hundred horsemen ride through the sentry-lines until in a loud voice comes the cry from the Irish commander, 'Sarsfield is the word and Sarsfield is the man!' And five hundred sabres are drawn, as the horsemen charge down on the sleeping convoy. It is all over in a few moments. The pontoons are smashed. The guns are filled with gunpowder, placed muzzle down in the earth, the wagons are piled in a circle round them, a train of gunpowder is set to them and the five hundred horsemen withdraw to watch the end of William's siege train.

With a flash and an explosion that awakens the villages for miles around, and is seen even in William's camp, the convoy is blown sky-high. In a few hours Sarsfield is welcomed back within the walls of Limerick.

But, alas, all Sarsfield's adventures were not to be so easy or so fortunate. William procured another siege train from Waterford. He broke the walls of Limerick near St John's Gate and sent ten thousand storm troops into the breach. The story of this fight is still told and sung in Ireland and it will never die. Wives and daughters joined their men-folk in the fight and beat back the enemy with anything that came to hand. Tradesmen snatched the muskets from the hands of wounded soldiers and carried on. Butchers leapt into the fight stabbing with their

long knives. Sticks, stones, scythes – anything that could be used to maim or kill – were used with deadly effect and for two terrible hours the fight swayed back and forth through the streets of Limerick. In the midst of the fighting a terrible explosion shook the city. William's Brandenburgers, a crack Prussian foot regiment, had been blown up in the powder magazine which they had captured. Three times the royalist armies flung themselves on Limerick; three times they were sent reeling back from the city walls. When night fell 2,000 of William's troops lay dead or dying.

That was the first siege of Limerick. Three days later William sailed for England. But the war in Ireland still went on.

There was that heroic battle on the bridge at Athlone. The royalist troops were attempting to ford the river.

'Are there ten men here who will die with me for Ireland?' cried Sergeant Costume of Maxwell's Irish Dragoons.

Ten men led by Costume sprang from their barricade and hacked at the pontoons with axes until one by one they fell under a hail of bullets. While these gallant men were dying another hero cried for volunteers, and again eleven men rushed out and hacked at the beams. Only two of these got back to their trenches.

On 25 August, the second siege of Limerick opened with a terrible cannonade from the Williamite forces. Limerick was now the last city in Ireland held by the Jacobites. Sarsfield was in command with the remnants of the Irish army. The city was surrounded, but it held out all through September. On 3 October an honourable peace was agreed on and the gallant defenders of Limerick surrendered. It was on the large slab of stone at the bridge head that Patrick Sarsfield signed the famous Treaty of

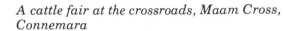

Limerick. The Irish were by this Treaty to enjoy full civil and religious liberty and all Irish soldiers who had fought for James were to be given a free passage to France.

Only a few days after the Truce was signed French reinforcements appeared in the Shannon: 4,000 trained troops and 10,000 arms with ammunition and provisions. But too late! General Ginkel, the head of the Williamite forces, was fearful lest Sarsfield would tear up the Treaty and resume the fight. He had nothing to fear.

'We have pledged our honour and the honour of Ireland,' said Sarsfield.

With drums beating and colours flying, the Irish forces marched out of Limerick into the great meadow on the Clare bank of the Shannon. King William, who was a soldier and knew troops when he met them, was anxious to enlist as many of Sarsfield's men as possible. Proclamations offering service in the English ranks were passed from hand to hand. There were 14,000 on this sad parade. Only 1,046 joined the English forces, 2,000 decided to retire to their farms and 11,000, with Sarsfield as their leader, lined up beneath the flag of France.

They had no sooner left the shores of Ireland than the Treaty was violated. King William was perhaps no more to blame for it than he was for the Massacre of Glencoe. The English Parliament had wrested from him the chief share in the domestic government of the country. Had Ireland's fate depended on the Crown and not on the Parliament it would have gone differently, for King William was an honourable soldier. Out of this gallant Irish sacrifice came only more Penal Laws directed against Catholics and the deliberate ruin of the Irish woollen trade. . . .

Meanwhile the 'Wild Geese' were flying over the world. Wherever England's enemies were to be found, Irish soldiers of misfortune would be in the front rank with them. It is said that from the time of the Treaty of Limerick in 1691 to the Battle of Fontenoy in 1745 no fewer than 450,000 Irishmen died in the service of France. The Irish Brigade is a remarkable event in the military history of the world. The Irish Catholics took their revenge for Limerick at Fontenoy; the Irish Protestants took their revenge for the wool embargo at the Battle of Bunker's Hill. Peace be upon this great and splendid army which although it fell upon foreign soil and in foreign quarrels knew that it died for Ireland.

Sarsfield was killed at the moment of victory during the battle of Landen on 29 July 1693. He was struck from his horse by a musket ball. As he lay wounded he heard the orders to advance. He knew that the English were falling back. He placed his hand on his breast and withdrew it wet with his blood. He looked at it and made one of the most splendid remarks in history.

'Oh,' he said sorrowfully, 'that this were for Ireland!'

But it was for Ireland. Sarsfield filled a place in Irish history comparable with that of William Wallace in the history of Scotland. He was not a tribal chieftain. The clans had been crushed and their leaders driven into the hills. But a new Ireland was arming herself for the fight; and he was its first leader.

In his last cry we seem to see clearly for the first time that Ireland of the Sorrows for whom so many brave men have suffered and died. He is one of the deathless characters in the history of nationalism: a great soldier, a man cast in the unhappy heroic mould, a noble patriot and a man of honour.

No land on earth has borne a nobler son than Patrick Sarsfield.

Ireland might be compared to a medieval castle which is being modernized and fitted with electricity. Half the rooms are unoccupied, and many of the turrets have not been entered for centuries, but – there must be an electric switch in each one of them! Will electricity bring the old castle to life again and fill it with paying guests?

That, briefly, is the problem of Ireland's mighty £5,000,000 Shannon power scheme, which is now making its electricity.* The most medieval country in Europe owns the most up-to-date electrical equipment in the world. Over the land of the small farmer, whose methods are those of ancient Babylon, now flashes the power of milking cows by electricity; over the white cabin whose inhabitants have never seen a bath is the possibility of heating water by pressing a button.

Everyone who desires to see Ireland a peaceful and prosperous nation will pray for the success of the Shannon scheme, because the future of Ireland is bound up with it. There are, of course, as usual in Ireland, two points of view. Some Irishmen say that cheap electricity broadcast over the land will in a few years make Ireland another Denmark; others say that the Irish farmer will not employ the power! Some say that an electric Ireland will develop thousands of new industries; others say that nothing will ever make Ireland an industrial nation!

* Editor's note. This is an excellent example of how H. V. Morton, in his light-hearted way, puts his finger on the issues which recur and endure in the countries he writes about.

Islanders carrying a curragh, Inisheer, Aran Islands

Galway harbour

A German engineer in a Norfolk jacket and tweed cycling knickers explained the scheme to me. The Shannon is being harnessed by German brains and Irish muscle. About 300 German engineers and foremen, and 4,000 Irish labourers, had been working on it since 1925.

He told me, with pride, that everything had come from Germany – 30,000 tons of machinery, 40,000 tons of coal, 8,000 tons of oil, 3,000 tons of iron, 400 tons of explosives for blasting the rock.

He gazed with pride over the amazing scene. We could hear the throbbing dynamos in the temporary station. They light the Shannon Valley from Killaloe and drive all the nightmare machines. . . .

'And what,' I asked, 'is Ireland to get out of this?'

'Foreign industry!' he replied instantly.

'You mean to say that there will be an invasion of foreign capital?'

'Well, why not? It will mean employment. It will reduce taxation. German factories will spring up. Belgian factories. Perhaps American factories. . . .'

'Poor Ireland!' I said. 'Can she never be alone?'

He looked at me as if I were mad. (The Shannon, by the way, has often been the main route for invasions of Ireland.)

'And the Irish farmer?' I asked.

'The Irish farmer?' he repeated, shrugging his shoulders.

'How much is the power to cost?'

'It is not known.'

I came over the mountains of Clare into the grey town of Galway as men were lighting lamps in the harbour. An unearthly afterglow lingered in the sky, a dull red haze hung over the hills

Seaweed for fertiliser, Co. Clare

Next page, left *Rossaveal, Co. Galway*

Next page, right *Salmon Weir Bridge, Co. Galway*

like the dust flung from chariot wheels, and the edges of the Atlantic were washed in a colour so strange and so vivid, almost a pale green, that melted marvellously into the blue of the dusk. And as the light was drawn out of the sky a few stars hung over the grape-blue heights of Connemara.

Such a velvet softness pervaded Galway, and in those first moments I felt, as one feels sometimes on meeting a stranger, that a new loyalty had come into life. Galway did not seem to belong to any part of Ireland that I have seen; it seemed to belong only to itself.

I know now that the strange beauty that flies like dust through Galway is the spirit of Gaelic Ireland, something that is a defiance to time, something that is like a declaration of faith. Galway must be almost too beautiful to an Irishman. He must feel about it as an Englishman would feel if, in an England conquered for centuries, and speaking a foreign tongue, he came one night to a little town in Somerset and heard men talking English.

When the hotel porter was unloading my luggage he drove away a determined old woman shrouded in a black shawl who was trying to tell me something. I went after her and asked her what she wanted. Her husband was out of work and her sons were out of work. She was a gentle old creature, and when I placed a shilling in her hand she said:

'May the Virgin bless you and bring you safe home.'

I encountered her twice during my first walk round Galway, and each time she repeated her blessing with a gratitude out of all proportion to the miserable gift, so that I felt that my first steps in the West were taken in sanctity. . . .

I went through many a narrow street, past a ruined Spanish house, for Galway reflects Spain in the eyes of its people, and, here and there, in a square house with a central courtyard and a gate flush with the street.

But what a town of yesterday! The curse of Cromwell lies heavier on Galway than on any other Irish town. It is a town of dead factories and great houses brought to decay. In the Middle Ages Galway was the Bristol of Ireland. Its very name has the ring of a great city in it – London, York, Bristol, Dublin, Galway; there is something high and authoritative about such names.

The fourteen Anglo-Norman families of Galway, who gained for their town the title of 'Galway of the Tribes', were the most exclusive families in Ireland. I believe that they inter-married for so long that special dispensation had more than once to be obtained to establish canonical legality. They founded the fortunes of the town. The quays were stacked with the wine casks of Spain. The galleons of Galway were as accustomed to the ports of Spain as they were to Irish waters. During the Civil War, Galway remained loyal to Charles, but Cromwell had his way with it in the end, and Galway has never recovered. Today the population of this once mighty seaport is reduced to that of a small English country town.

I met an Irishman in the hotel who told me this story: 'During the war a German submarine appeared in the bay and the captain gave orders to bombard Galway. A young officer who was making a reconnaissance sent down the message: "Galway *has* been bombarded, sir." '

My friend thought this was a screamingly funny story; but I could not laugh at it.

I was lucky enough to meet a little pink-faced, middle-aged Irishman known to everyone as Michael John. If you have ever fished in Galway you will know him well!

We went round the town together, to the
Church of St Nicholas, patron saint of children,
sailors (and thieves!), where a bell hangs taken
(no one knows how or why) from an abbey in
France; we went to gaze at an old Spanish house
in which the term 'lynching' and 'lynch law'
originated; and Michael John told me the grim
story.

In 1493 John Lynch FitzStephen, Mayor of
Galway, went over to Spain to improve trade
relations between that country and Galway. He
was entertained by a rich merchant named
Gomez, whose son, a handsome young Spaniard,
returned to Ireland as his guest. Lynch had a
son named Walter, and the two young men
became friends. Walter Lynch was in love with
a girl named Agnes, whose father, a merchant of
Galway, spoke Spanish perfectly, and was
delighted to welcome the young Spaniard to his
house. Walter Lynch became madly jealous,
and one day, in the height of his passion, he
stabbed the Spaniard and threw his body in the
sea.

Walter Lynch was arrested and confessed his
guilt. His father, as mayor, pronounced the
death sentence. But no man in Galway would
execute the boy! The mob attempted a rescue,
but before this could be made, and in sight of the
crowd, Lynch hanged his own son. (There is
another version which traces the origin of
'lynch law' to South Carolina in the nineteenth
century, but Galway has not heard of this.)

'I suppose he felt he had to do it,' said Michael
John, 'for the honour of Galway. His son had
not only committed murder, he had violated the
laws of hospitality. After the hanging Lynch
went to his home, and was never seen again by
living man. . . .'

It is by the strangest perversion of meaning

that 'lynch law' means today the vengeance by a mob on a criminal.

We went to the salmon weir on Galway River, which Michael John knows as a man knows his own land.

'A little later in the year,' he said, 'this is the most surprising sight in Ireland. You can look down from the bridge and see great salmon, thirty- and forty-pounders, packed as tight as sardines in a tin! You wouldn't believe it unless you saw it! Back to back they are, waiting like a great crowd at a ticket office to get up to the lakes from the sea. . . .'

This narrow river is the only entrance from the sea to 1,200 miles of lakes.

I suppose the river by Galway Weir is the angler's paradise. They tell a story of a fisherman who died from excitement here, but they do not end the story with the funniest part of it. The local paper, after reporting the event, said: 'Our readers will be glad to learn that the rod which Mr —— dropped was immediately taken up by our esteemed townsman, Mr ——,

who found the fish still on, and after ten minutes' play succeeded in landing it – a fine, clean-run salmon of fifteen pounds.'

That, I am sure, is the perfect epitaph!

We went over the dangerous wooden weir above the rushing water, and were just in time to see a man with a boathook murder an amazing salmon which turned the scale at forty-two pounds! He was as big as a shark and thick. Two nets are out for salmon, but a clear passage must be left by law. A fish gets caught by sheer bad luck or natural foolishness. Every weekend the nets are lifted, also by law, so that a sensible salmon should come up from the sea on a Sunday.

'What do you do with salmon?' I said to the man who was weighing the monster.

'London,' he replied briefly.

I know now where the world ends.

It is a grey land, and the gold clouds ride up over the edge of it, shouldering one another, slow as a herd of steers. The land is as grey and speckled as a piece of homespun tweed. It is grey with hundreds and thousands of little stone walls. They run up to the edge of the sky, and they fall into dips and hollows, criss-crossing like the lines of your hand. These grey walls guard the smallest 'fields' in the world. They are not real fields: they are just bits of rocks sprinkled with soil. Some of them are no larger than a dining-table, some of them are oblong, some square, some almost circular, some triangular; and to every one is its own little breast-high wall, so that the land, silver-grey wherever you look, is, as I say, just like a big piece of the tweed that they weave in the hills.

The white road twists like a snake between the grey walls, and over it walk strong, barelegged girls. They swing from the hips as they walk with the grace of those who have never known shoe leather, and they carry on their backs great loads of brown seaweed in wicker baskets. Or they ride, sitting sideways with their bare legs to the road, above the tails of placid donkeys, over whose backs are slung baskets piled with peat.

Behind the grey land, moving round in a solemn dance as you go over the twisting road, are blue hills – hills blue as the sea at Capri – with the biggest and the most golden clouds on earth like haloes over their heads. Among the blue hills and the grey fields, and beside the blue waters of little loughs and on the edges of sudden peat bogs, stand small cabins, incredibly poor and marvellously white, with hens round the door pecking round fat black pots.

And the sound of this land is the click of a donkey's hoofs on the road and the ring of a spade like a crowbar which men drive into the rocky soil. When the sun goes out this place is as grey as a ghost.

Connemara. . . .

How can it exist in the modern world! In years of travel I have seen nothing like it. It begins suddenly as soon as you leave Galway due west by the coast road through Spiddal to Clifden. It is a part of the earth in which Progress – whatever we mean by it – has broken in vain against grey walls; it has been arrested by high hills and deep lakes to the east and by the sea on the west. These people have been locked away for centuries by geography and poverty. I have been into the tomb of Tutankhamen in Egypt, but entering Connemara gave me a finer feeling of discovery and a greater sense of remoteness from modern life!

They are so poor that no one has ever tried to exploit them; their land is so poor that no one has ever tried to steal it. There are no railways, no shops, no motor-cars. There are three things only: the Catholic Faith, Nature, and work.

Connemara could not be more astonishing than the discovery in England of a forgotten country in which men spoke the language of Bede or Alfred the Great, wore Saxon clothes, and prayed to Saxon saints. Connemara is the most surprising thing in the British Isles. It is nearer to St Patrick than it is to Dublin.

Near the coast I saw drawn up outside cabins or leaning against grey walls, the queer canoes, called curraghs, in which the fishermen of Connemara dare the perils of the ocean; and dare must be the right and only word! They are light as feathers, and made of skins or canvas stretched over a wooden frame. They are exactly the same as the coracles used by the Ancient Britons in the time of Caesar.

A few miles farther on I saw a man making a 'field'! The mystery of the stone walls was solved! They are not so much a sign of ownership as a necessary preliminary to a 'field'. The whole of Connemara in ancient times must have been subjected to a fall of stones the size of a man's head. A 'field' is made by gathering up these stones and making a wall of them round the rock from which they have been removed! (Do any people on earth scratch a living from more villainous soil?)

While I watched him a big, dark girl sprang over a stone wall and walked over the sharp rocks in her bare feet with a basket of earth on her back. This she poured on the cleared rock, laughed a moment with the man, and, taking up her basket, leapt over the wall again like a deer.

I went on down the road. Grey walls; white cabins; little chapels, so small, many of them, that when the people tramp in for miles on Sunday morning the priests celebrate Mass in the open. But always grey walls and little poor fields spread with seaweed. I saw a lovely thing on a hill. Children poured out of a small corrugated iron school. The hill rang with laughter. They danced round in a circle, their little bare legs flashing in the sunlight, and in the centre of them, wind-blown, tall, slim, was a young girl, the teacher.

I watched the sun sink into the sea at evening, and I saw night fall over the grey land at the world's end. And I knew then the strangeness that blows through the town of Galway like dust.

That town is half in the world and half out of it. It is a frontier post, and the winds from the end of the world blow into it day and night.

In the centre of a 'field' a piece of ground higher than the rest has never been levelled. A thorn bush grows on its summit. The farmer who owns this useless and heart-breaking land has cultivated all round the tiny hill, leaving the hillock to sprout weeds and thorns. The reason why he has done this is simple and well known. The high ground is a fort or rath. The people say that such forts were built by the Danes. Some people think that this word is a corrupted form of De Danann, the mysterious people called Tuatha de Danann – 'the tribes of the Goddess Danu'. They are said to have conquered Ireland by virtue of great magic. But the druids of the people of Mil were too strong for them; and magic meeting magic, Tuatha de Danann were forced to fly and take refuge in the fairy mounds.

Every countryman in the West of Ireland knows that these places are haunted. It is on record that a labourer gave up the land which he had secured under the Labourers Act and upon which a well-disposed district council was willing to build him a house because, as he wrote to the council, 'on no account would he interfere with the fairies' home'.

That is why in the West you see so many raths with their trees waving above them, the standards of an invisible world; and all round the meagre crops are growing but never intruding on the territory that belongs to fairyland.

'What are the fairies?' Padraic Colum asked a blind man whom he met on a West of Ireland road.

His face filled with an intensity of conviction.

'The fairies,' he said. 'I will tell you who the fairies are. God moved from His seat, and when He turned round Lucifer was in it. Then Hell was made in a minute. God moved His hand and swept away thousands of angels. And it was in

His mind to sweep away thousands more. "O God Almighty, stop!" said Angel Gabriel. "Heaven will be swept clean out." "I'll stop," said God Almighty; "them that are in Heaven, let them remain in Heaven; them that are in Hell, let them remain in Hell; and them that are between Heaven and Hell, let them remain in the air." And the Angels that remained between Heaven and Hell are the Fairies.'

What he said was as true to the man as one of the Gospels.

Saxon fairies are naughty children like Puck, who loved to turn the milk sour and knock fat women from their milking stools. In Scotland the fairies are sinister and terrible. I have talked to men who have seen Highland fairies. I know a young man who drives the village hearse in a lochside village in the far north. He sees fairies and 'ghost lights' before anyone dies, and, being a practical youth, he at once cleans up the hearse! But these Scottish fairies are mostly terrible. A Scotsman would kill a fairy as he would kill a stoat.

W. B. Yeats commented on this. He attributes it to the stern theological character of the Scot, which has made 'even the devil religious'. But in Ireland the people have settled down in kindly tolerance side by side with their old gods, which is, of course, what all fairies are.

'Our Irish fairy terrors have about them something of make-believe,' writes W. B. Yeats. 'When a peasant strays into an enchanted hovel, and is made to turn a corpse all night on a spit before the fire, we do not feel anxious; we know he will wake in the midst of a green field, the dew on his old coat.'

This graciousness to fairies is, I think, all part of the aristocratic hospitality of Ireland. Only mean and low-born people are ungracious to a guest. In the old days when heroes walked the world disguised as common men – just as Ulysses came home from his wanderings – you never knew for whom you poured wine or broke bread. Your common harper might rise up and, casting off his rags, become a god.

And on the roads of Connemara I feel as though I am in Ancient Greece, and that men know that a stranger with all the mystery and potentialities of a stranger is abroad upon the roads. They look at me with a gentle yet searching interest, as though I might be an old god playing a trick in a tweed coat.

If this were so, and a wandering god from the old times came to them and proved himself, they would not, I think, betray him to the priest. They would take him in, sorry for him and vaguely proud of him also; and they would give him milk and kill a fowl for him and go short of potatoes in order to feed him. Not until he was far off down the road beyond the wrath of men would they, I am sure, go to confession!

I talked to a young fisherman who had brought ashore a pot full of blue lobsters.

'Will you sell one to me?' I asked.

I had an idea that I might take the lobster to my next hotel and ask them to cook it, not as a test of Irish manners, but because I can seldom resist lobster.

The young man replied that he would like to sell me a lobster, but he was not at liberty to do so. He worked for a man who sold all the lobsters caught in the neighbourhood so that they did not belong to him but to his master.

'To whom does he sell them?'

He said that French trawlers called for them at regular intervals.

I stood there on a slippery rock wondering how many times I have sat in a Paris hotel, a

View from the roof of Bunratty Castle, Co. Clare, with the River Shannon in the background

Next page *Cottages at Leenane, Co. Galway*

string orchestra playing and a *maître d'hôtel* leaning forward with a religious expression and a poised pencil, saying:

'The lobsters are – magnificent!'

I could not help laughing.

The young man looked hurt and embarrassed, so that I hastened to explain.

'I think it rather funny that I should have to go to Paris to eat one of your lobsters.'

He did not think it at all funny, because it meant nothing at all to him; but he flung back his head and laughed as a compliment to my sense of humour.

But it is rather odd. I shall never eat lobster in Paris again but I shall see the Atlantic sweeping into the fretted coast of Connemara, a little cloud sitting on the head of a blue hill, and I shall hear in imagination the young fisherman's voice and the sound of yellow seaweed popping in the warm sun.

Connemara to Paris. . . .

It is hardly possible to believe that two such places could have any traffic one with the other, or even that they can exist in the same world.

The one-room cabin lies a mile or so from the road over a hill; and inside live a man, a woman, and eight children. The next cabin, which is rare in this district, is three miles away, and the nearest shop, such as it is, ten. They are in the backwoods of Connemara. This family is linked to the world of men only by a belief in God, otherwise they would be as lost as mountain sheep without a shepherd.

As it is, they are a lonely outpost of Christian culture – if that is not too strong a word – rather like a wild flower springing in the footprint of a saint. They live in the Shadow of God. They talk about Him as though He helped them that morning to bake the soda-bread in the peat-embers, and was with them last night to drive the pig in from the perils of the peat-bog.

St Columba, who left Ireland 1,365 years ago to convert the North of England, is a greater reality to them than any living man. They talk about him with the circumstantial detail of eye-witnesses, so that at first you think they are describing someone they encountered last week in the hills. They tell you how he cured his mother's toothache and how he rebuked his son that day when they were driving back cows from the fair at Ballyhean – simple stories made up by them and their fathers on the hillside or round the fire at night, and repeated so often that they have become true.

They live in a cruel beauty, for the wildness around them was never meant to give food or shelter to man or beast. Their consumptive-looking cow roams the rock sadly in search of herbage, a poor scapegoat creature, lean as a rake, and their three potato-patches, none larger than a small carpet, are dotted about the landscape, ten minutes' walk one from the other, because only in these patches does some geological crack or seam permit the presence of a thin soil.

They are so used to insufficient food that hunger is fortunately something they do not notice. . . .

But if you offered to remove them to better land in another county they would fight you with pitchforks to the death!

The man is a mystery. He is not aware that I know he 'did' six months' recently, for making poteen. They caught him red-handed one misty day in the hills – fell right on him, in fact – as he was brewing 'the stuff' over peat in a cave. Prison has left no mark on him. I suppose he just sat in his cell thinking about St Columba – or

Columcille as he calls him in Irish.

I have never seen a more ragged man. His trousers are unbelievable. He must have owned and inherited perhaps twenty pairs during his life, every one of which is represented in the present astonishing garment. If he fell asleep in the hills, I am sure the leprechauns would come out and play chess on him!

Like all his tribe, he is gentle, well-mannered, with thoughtful, dark eyes, and a thin, high nose. There is a stray touch of decayed aristocracy about him. The first time you see him you think: 'Hullo, what an old tramp!' and you address him gruffly, anticipating roughness, but when he replies courteously with a smile and a well-turned sentence you feel abashed and apologetic!

How he keeps his large family I do not know. (Perhaps they keep themselves.) He appears to sit about all day on a big stone, smoking his pipe, looking round the hills, waiting apparently for something that never happens. . . .

I wonder if the peat-bog could tell a different story . . . but, let us change the subject, and meet his wife!

The cabin is dark because the windows, which are set high up, are no larger than sheets of foolscap, and everything in it smells of peat. A peat-fire, that has not gone out probably for centuries, burns with a clear vermilion flame and powders into white ash as fine as talc. Above this fire hangs a big black pot. On the wall are pictures of the Holy Family and the Flight into Egypt.

The woman kneels on the earth floor, rocking a cradle in which peeps the monkey face of a five-month-old infant; round her crawl and climb, bubble and dribble, three babies between the ages of one, two and four years. Two bigger boys are at school. Two strapping girls, one twelve and the other fourteen, are vaguely useful about the place, slapping an infant out of the fire, stirring the black pot, or taking a turn at the cradle.

The mother of this hearty tribe is about thirty-six, but she looks quite fifty. Beauty seems to fly in a night in Connemara. It is distressing to see lovely young girls aged by hard work in the twenties, and by lack of care and insufficient food. This woman has been romantically beautiful, and even now, with care, kindness, flattery, a visit to a dentist, a hairdresser, a dressmaker and a bathroom she would still be attractive. She belongs to that thin, whipcord Latin type, and her big eyes, dark, gentle and warm, with long centuries in the depth of them, look straight into you.

The most earnest social reformer could not patronize these people. There is no class barrier to negotiate. There is grim poverty, but not the squalid poverty of a slum; it is not pitiful poverty, because these people feel no self-pity.

Outside on a stone the head of the family sits smoking and watching the clouds roll up over the hills. We talk of the difficulty of growing food in such a spot. He says that he is, thanks to God, better off than many a man. Over there, now – he points with his pipe across the hills to the sea – men live on the edge of rocks and carry the seaweed all day and even the earth in wicker baskets. . . .

'But they love their rocks?'

'They do,' he says, 'and it's not leaving they'd be, if you gave them all the Plain o' Meath! But 'tis starvation!'

'Yet they are happy?'

'Aye, it's happy they are, sure enough, but – 'tis just starvation!'

That seems to me to sum up Connemara! But, for the life of me, I cannot pity them!

Inisheer, Aran Islands

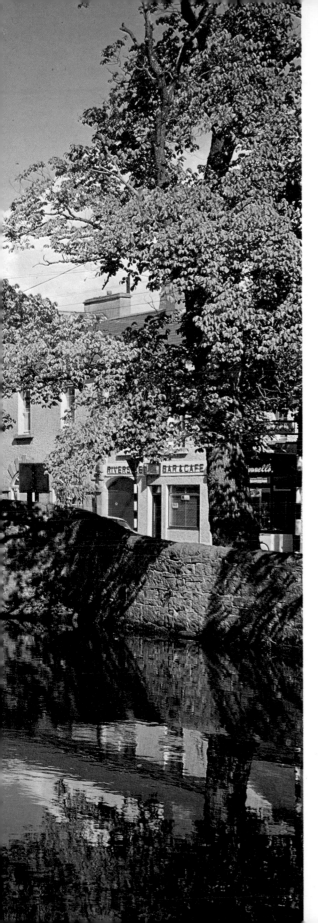

5
CROAGH PATRICK TO TARA

Clifden, the capital of Connemara, lies in the shadow of the Twelve Pins. These mountains are among the most fascinating that I have ever seen. They dominate the landscape in Connemara, now to your left and again to your right as you move through this country; sometimes the clouds swing low and decapitate them; often, especially at evening, they stand up in a sky blue as the Bay of Naples.

Clifden is a small, clean, stone-built town with one wide main street. The hill on which it is built slopes to an estuary that points straight out over the Atlantic to America.

It was strange to make contact with the outside world in the hotel. Here were fishermen with the accents of Dublin and England. The most interesting person, however, was a chauffeur whom I met at the bar; rather, his story was interesting. He asked me if I had noticed an elderly American at luncheon. I had. A thin, sallow man who wore horn spectacles.

'That's himself,' said the chauffeur; and there was something sympathetic and kindly in his attitude.

He told me in that dramatic narrative manner which most Irishmen possess that as soon as a certain liner had docked at Cobh this American rushed to the garage where the young chauffeur worked, and chartered a car to take him to a little town in County Mayo. He explained that he wanted to 'run up' to see his brother and then rush back and catch the next boat to America.

On the journey north from Cork to Mayo there was plenty of time for my companion's honeyed tongue. And the American, proving not so sallow and uncommunicative as he looked, told the Irishman a lot about himself and his mission. He had emigrated from Mayo thirty years previously. For years his con-

Next page *Westport Bay, showing Croagh Patrick*

science had pricked him because, in spite of success, he had never been home to see his elder brother, whose tragedy it was to stay in Ireland to inherit an uneconomic farm. He had returned at last and was about to pay a surprise visit to his brother.

Unlike every American previously encountered by this chauffeur, he was a 'terrible teetotaller entirely'. He even kept a keen eye on his driver, and when once, at Limerick, the young man had been discovered with his face in a pint of porter the American had lectured him sternly, ordering him to abstain from all liquor while in his service.

They arrived in the town in Mayo and the American was appropriately affected. He made his way to the old home, opened the door, but a strange face greeted him:

'Will it be old Pat Murphy ye want – him that keeps the saloon?'

'The saloon?' cried the American, horrified and indignant.

'Aye; that's himself. . . .'

They went to Pat Murphy's saloon in the little street. There, sure enough, was the favourite brother sitting up behind the counter fast asleep. The American's heart melted at the sight so that he forgot the smell of stale drink that haunts all Irish saloons.

'Pat!' he said, going round and shaking him gently. 'Pat, do ye know who's here?'

For answer Pat gave a grunt and slid gently to the floor, dead drunk.

'And he stood there and looked at him a while,' said the chauffeur; 'then he turned on his heel and he said, "Take me back to Cork. It's the next boat I'll be catching. . . ."'

The young man drank up and put his cap straight.

Donegal Castle

'An' niver a word has he given me from that time to this,' he said. 'And to think a man would come all the way from America for that. He's a hard man entirely,' I'm thinking. Still, it's sorry for him I am, taking it to heart the way he does. . . .'

I watched the American get into the motorcar and sit there with the set face of a Puritan elder.

Behind the Twelve Pins lies the lovely mountain country of the Joyces. This was a family of Welsh descent which settled in this part of the West by permission of the dominant O'Flahertys in the last year of the thirteenth century.

Connemara lives on the sea and the fruits of the sea, but the people of the Joyce Country live upon the mountain. Their active little sheep graze on the splendid uplands, and the wool is taken from them, washed, and spun in the cottages on the hillsides and made into Irish tweed on hand-looms. It would be easy to confound the Joyce Country with Connemara; they exist side by side on the map, but a difference not only of clan separates them: the vast difference in all the ways of life that separates fishermen from mountaineers.

The journey from Clifden through Letterfrack to Leenane is, I think, one of the most perfect scenes in the West of Ireland. I went along this road on a bright day with the sea intensely blue and huge golden clouds sailing above the crests of the hills. Ahead of me, dominating the scene, was the highest mountain of the north-west – Muilrea – and next to him was Ben Bury and Benlugmore, three monsters that rise up into the sky from an arm of the sea.

Leenane lies among the mountains on the

edge of a great fiord called Killary Harbour. Connemara is now a dream. The country has changed. The great hills slope up to barren summits, and the sound is not that of a spade hitting the rock but the bleating of sheep and the clack of a shuttle. Near the post office is a wooden shed where all day long a hand-loom bumps and bangs as the wool from the Joyce Country sheep is turned into homespun. It is a finer, closer tweed than that of Kerry; in fact, rather like Donegal, but lacking the sudden specks of colour: excellent hard stuff with the colour of the Joyce Country in it.

As I went on round the eastern limit of Killary Harbour I saw five young men pulling in a salmon net. They formed a group that might have come from the very dawn of the world. They wore homespun tweed. Their sleeves were rolled above their muscular elbows. Their necks were baked red with wind and sun. As they pulled they shouted to one another in Gaelic; and slowly the great net was hauled in to shore.

It was an exciting moment. I nearly broke my neck scrambling down to the water's edge to be in time to see it. As the net was pulled slowly towards the bank, the water, perhaps fifteen yards out, suddenly boiled with furious life, the sun shone on four feet of living silver as the great fish leapt and lashed in the net. The men sang out in their excitement and pulled, one directing them in Gaelic. The salmon leapt up into the sunlight. I saw the whole of him; a silver monster, an eighteen-pounder with great shoulders on him and a tail with the kick of a mule in it.

It was a moment I shall never forget: the sun on the opposite hills; the scent of wild thyme; the splashing at the water's edge; the Gaelic shouts that sounded like war-cries; the bright,

leaping body in the net: over it all the simple splendour of a lost world.

When Lent came in the year A.D. 449 St Patrick retired to a great mountain in Connaught to commune with God. He fasted there for forty days and forty nights, weeping, so it is said, until his chasuble was wet with tears.

The medieval monks possessed detailed accounts of St Patrick's fast. They said that to the angel, who returned to him every night with promises from God, the saint said:

'Is there aught else that will be granted to me?'

'Is there aught else thou wouldst demand?' asked the angel.

'There is,' replied St Patrick, 'that the Saxons shall not abide in Ireland by consent or perforce so long as I abide in heaven.'

'Now get thee gone,' commanded the angel.

'I will not get me gone,' said St Patrick, 'since I have been tormented until I am blessed.'

'Is there aught else thou wouldst demand?' asked the angel once more.

St Patrick requested that on the Day of Judgment he should be judge over the men of Ireland.

'Assuredly,' said the angel, 'that is not got from the Lord.'

'Unless it is got from Him,' replied the determined saint, 'departure from this Rick shall not be got from me from today until Doom; and, what is more, I shall leave a guardian there.'

The angel returned with a message from heaven:

'The Lord said, "There hath not come, and there will not come from the Apostles, a man more admirable, were it not for thy hardness.

What thou hast prayed for thou shalt have . . . and there will be a consecration of the men of the folk of Ireland, both living and dead."'

St Patrick said:

'A blessing on the bountiful King who hath given; and the Rick shall now be departed therefrom.'

As he arose and prepared to descend from the mountain mighty birds flew about him so that the air was dark and full of the beating of wings. So St Patrick stood, like Moses on Sinai, and round him all the Saints of Ireland, past, present, and to come.

In this we can see the Irish belief in the inflexible determination of their saint: 'a steady and imperturbable man'. And it was said that while upon this mountain in Connaught St Patrick banished all snakes from Ireland.

This mountain, Croagh Patrick – or Patrick's Hill – lifts its magnificent cone 2,510 feet above the blue waters of Clew Bay. It is Ireland's Holy Mountain. Once a year in July a pilgrimage is made to the little chapel on the crest. Atlantic liners drop anchor in Galway Bay, bringing Irish-Americans who wish to ascend the mountain for the good of their souls. As many as 40,000 pilgrims have climbed the mountain in one day; and many of the more devout remove their shoes and socks and take the hard path barefoot.

The morning broke dangerously clear and fine. I took a stout stick and prepared to climb the mighty flank of Ireland's Sinai. As I approached it, admiring the high pattern of wheeling clouds over its head, I could see far off the little Mass chapel like a cairn of stones on the crest.

I plodded on over a rough mountain path worn by the feet of the faithful century after

Sunset at Westport, Co. Mayo

Opposite page *Grace O'Malley Castle, Achill Sound, Co. Mayo*

Next page, left *Muireadach's Cross, Monasterboice, Co. Louth*

Next page, right *Clifden, Connemara*

century. A wind blew in from the Atlantic bringing rain with it, and in a few moments the earth was hidden in a thin grey mist. I was disappointed, but went on in the hope that the sky would clear in time and give me what must surely be the grandest view in Ireland.

There are few experiences more uncanny than climbing a mountain in mist and rain. As I went on and up, the mist grew thicker, and the drizzle fell in that peculiar persistent Irish way that wets you to the skin before you are aware of it. Above me was this grey wet pall, below me the same mystery; only the rocks under my feet were real, and there was no sound but the falling of water and the click of a dislodged stone rolling behind me down the path.

There is something terrifying, at least to me, in the mists that cover mountains – mists that hide you know not what; mists that cut a man off from the world and deny him the sight of the sky. To be lost on a mountain in mist is to experience all the horror of panic, for it seems to you that you might lose the path and go wandering vainly in circles answered only by a mocking laugh which seems to hide in all mountain mists. But I consoled myself by the thought that Croagh Patrick is a holy mountain from whose ravines and gullies all demons have been banished. Suddenly, right before me rose a white figure, and I looked up to a statue of St Patrick.

The saint, I discovered, stands there to hearten pilgrims, for the real climb begins behind him. The path ends. The climber ascends, picking his way over a steep gully, the loose stones sliding beneath his feet; and as I went on the joy of climbing in rain came to me, so that I loved the wetness of my cheeks and hair and the movement of the mist which told

me that I was in a great cloud that hid Croagh Patrick from the eyes of men.

I came to a cairn of stones: one of the Stations of the Cross. And as I stood there asking my Catholic ancestors what to do about it I heard a voice, and out of the mist came an unlikely and preposterous sight. A middle-aged woman was painfully descending the path. She looked exactly as though someone had taken her up in the very moment of buying six yards of *crépe de Chine* at a Grafton Street draper's and had blown her on top of Croagh Patrick. No sooner had she become startlingly clear in the narrow circle of my vision than another figure materialized from the mist: her husband. He also was incredible. He wore a bowler hat. It seemed so odd to encounter a bowler hat on a holy mountain. We said what a bad day it was. They asked if there were any more people coming up behind me. They told me it was their first pilgrimage. The woman was worried. She had lost a rosary among the stones. If I found it would I post it to her in Limerick? I thought how strange it was to English eyes: two solid, middle-aged people of the comfortable kind going off together to pray on the summit of a holy mountain.

'God be with you and bless you,' they said gravely; and I went on into the damp cloud.

Onward in the mist I went, hot and weary and happy; once I thought I had found the lost rosary, but it was only a piece of torn shoe-lace that had fallen into a hollow of the rocks. I passed another Station of the Cross and soon found myself on the peak of Croagh Patrick, 2,510 feet above Connaught, with the mountains of Mayo north of me, the blue Atlantic west of me, and south the mountains of the Joyce Country and the Twelve splendid Pins of

Achill Sound, Co. Mayo

Connemara. But, alas, not one glimmer of it shone through the wet cloud that hung over the holy mountain. . . .

On the summit of this height is a little Mass chapel. I was told in Connemara how this building was made. Cement in seven-pound bags was carted to the foot of the mountain and every pilgrim regarded it as an act of devotion to carry one of these to the top. Many a man, I was told, made the ascent more than once for the honour of carrying up material for the construction of this tiny oratory.

I went inside and knelt down. The place was very small and ice-cold. A young priest knelt in prayer. The wind howled round the little building in soft gusts, and I wondered what it felt like to be there in the great storms that swept in from the Atlantic. Even though the walls of the little chapel cut off the sight of moving mists there was something in the air of the chapel that told of a chilly solitude far from the comfortable earth. I was conscious that, outside, the mountain mists were sweeping past; the cold air told of a remote solitude; the rudeness of the little sanctuary was that of a shrine built on an outpost of the world. The kneeling priest never moved. He might have been carved in stone. He reminded me of some knight keeping vigil before the altar.

It was on this height, as told by the medieval monks, that St Patrick flung his bell from him only to have it returned to his hand; and at each sound of the bell the toads and the adders fled from Ireland. . . .

I went down over the wet stones. I came gratefully to the white statue of the saint. I had left the clouds above me, but the rain was falling, blotting out the sea and the hills.

Westport House, Co. Mayo

From Clew Bay, you can see, lying out perhaps four miles from the nearest land, a small green island called Clare Island.

On the shore facing the mainland is the ruined tower of Grace O'Malley's Castle. Legend says that this remarkable Irishwoman was buried on the island in an abbey which now, like her stronghold, is a ruin.

Grace O'Malley – or Granuaile as she is known in song and legend – was a kind of feminine Rob Roy of Ireland. History says little about her, but what little it says is exciting. She was a unique character.

When Queen Elizabeth was ruling England with the help of her astute councillors, Grace O'Malley was ruling the seaboard of Connaught by sheer force of character. She is without parallel in history: a sea-queen or a she-pirate. Her father was Owen O'Malley, called

Dhubdara – 'of the Black Oak'. His authority extended from the sea-coast to Aran, where he was Lord of the Isles. The clan had from the earliest days been famous for its daring deeds by sea, and the old chief was accompanied on many of his piratical voyages by his daughter. When he died she was a girl of nineteen. She had a younger brother, but, like Hatshepsut of Egypt, she calmly set him aside and declared her intention of becoming the chief of the clan. No one knows the composition of her fleet. She must have possessed certain wooden vessels, but no doubt the bulk of her navy was composed of coracles. Her stronghold, Carrigahowly Castle, was built at the edge of the water on Clare Island, and legend says that the young she-pirate was in the habit of mooring her navy and tying it together, then passing the main rope through a hole in her castle walls, retiring

On the road to Horn Head, Co. Donegal

Sculpture on a cross at Monasterboice, Co. Louth

to rest at night with the rope wound round her arm in order to be up and doing at the first alarm.

She lived in an age of piracy. It was the age of Francis Drake. The Spanish galleons which came up the west coast of Ireland with their wine cargoes for Galway were rich prey for her, but, like a good Gael, her chief attacks were made against the merchant ships of Elizabeth. She became so notorious that the English Government proclaimed her an outlaw and offered what in those days was an enormous sum, £500, for her capture. Troops stationed at Galway were sent to take her castle, but after a fortnight's siege they retired, and Queen Grace was left in peace.

Her first husband was O'Donnell O'Flaherty 'of the Wars' – evidently a fit mate for her – head of the 'ferocious' O'Flahertys. A record of her about this time is contained in a manuscript preserved in the Dublin archives:

She was a great pirate and plunderer from her youth. It is Transcended to us by Tradition that the very Day she was brought to bed of her first child, that a Turkish Corsair attacked her ships, and that they were getting the Better of Her Men, she got up, put the quilt about her and a string about her neck, took two Blunder Bushes in her hands, came on deck, began damning and capering about, her monstrous size and odd figure surprised the Turks, their officers gathered together talking of her. This was what she wanted. She stretched both her hands, fired the two Blunder Bushes at them and Destroyed the officers.

That was the sort of woman she was!

When O'Flaherty died she chose as her second husband a powerful Anglo-Norman named Sir Richard Bourke, known to his Irish sept as MacWilliam Eughter. His personal nickname was 'Richard in Iron', an allusion to the plate armour which he wore. Grace, it is said, insisted on observing a companionate marriage. If after twelve months the marriage was not satisfactory either party to it should have the power to dissolve it. Some reports say that she employed the companionate year to the garrisoning of her husband's strongholds along the coast, and at the end of it closed the gates of her castle upon him and declared the marriage ended.

We touch surer ground, however, in 1576, when Grace O'Malley went to Galway to ask Sir Henry Sidney to accept her fleet of three galleys and 200 men in the service of England. The upshot of her alliance with England was the most surprising event of all; she was invited by Elizabeth to visit London.

This visit took place in 1593, after the sea-queen had spent years in chasing the enemies of England up and down the Connaught coast. Tradition says that the queen and her retinue sailed to England and anchored in the Thames below old London Bridge. There are many accounts of the interview, which, some say, took place in Hampton Court Palace. The meeting of Elizabeth with the dark-haired she-pirate of Connaught must have been one of the most striking audiences of a picturesque reign. She announced herself as 'Grainne O'Malley, daughter of Doodarro O'Malley sometime chief of the country called Upper Owle O'Malley, now called the Barony of Murrasky'.

Unfortunately the end of this tempestuous and heroic figure was tame. She was buried in Clare Abbey, where, I am told, for many years her skull decorated with ribbons was shown to

147

visitors. But the story goes that in the nine-teenth century a company was formed in Scotland for the acquisition of bones for manure. A ship was fitted out which raided the West of Ireland, where immense quantities of bones were piled up in churchyards and old abbeys. Grania's bones, so they say, went to manure a Scottish acre.

There is, of course, an artistic Irish ending to this story. They say that one of Grania's grinders, discovered in a turnip, choked a Scotsman!

Seven thousand people, connected to Ireland by a narrow bridge, live on the Isle of Achill in the shadow of blue mountains and in the gloom of brown peat bogs. They think in Irish, and they speak Irish. When the sun shines they inhabit a paradise of colours. Titian-blue hills, blue skies, seas that rival the blue of Naples; but in bad weather the Atlantic waves scream on every side of them, and the winds from the east go tearing round the mountains like forty thousand devils.

Their little white cabins cluster incredibly on rock ledges; their small potato patches are scratched with heroic industry in the hard rock. They love dancing and music. The sound of their fiddles is like the twittering of sparrows. And they are all in debt to the grocer!

There is no money to be made in Achill, so that twelve months' credit is the easy-going custom. The whole island lives on credit.

What a strange, pathetic island! Yet none seems conscious of this. God has planted them on a sea-girt rock, therefore God intended them to remain there! Who would dare to murmur against the divine wisdom? The soil is hard.

There is no money. But one can earn money in the foreign countries of England and Scotland, situated, also it seems by divine providence, a few short hours off in a boat.

It is not strange to those who have seen the West of Ireland that contact with the great towns and cities of England and Scotland, generation after generation, should have left no mark on Achill. These people are superb conservatives. They appear to be immune from modern infections.

When the men go to foreign lands Achill becomes an isle of women. They run the home and they work the fields. They strive and plan for the return of their men in the autumn.

These women and the neurotic women of cities belong to different worlds. It is tragic to see beauty withering visibly and so early under the trials of a hard life. Here a woman is old at thirty and senile at forty. She knows nothing of comfort and care as women in cities know them, and there seems to be no time in her life when she can fold her hands and gaze about her from the privileged harbour of old age. You will see women labouring in the fields, and coming like beasts of burden along the road, but so bent and so wrinkled that their age defies supposition.

Yet there is laughter in Achill. The young girls laugh as they drive the geese over the rocks; they laugh as they climb the low stone walls with their baskets; they laugh as they call off the wild dogs that threaten to devour the stranger; they laugh most of all, so I am told, on evenings at dance time when the men are home from overseas and the fiddles twitter over the hills of Achill like birds under an eave.

The priest, sitting by a turf fire nursing his neuritis, says that the people are good people; and the doctor (who is the only other distin-guished resident) administers to the ills of

Joyce's River, Co. Galway

The north side of the Franciscan Moyne Abbey, Co. Mayo

Achill in a little makeshift surgery in the local inn and says that he would not exchange his life for the best practice in Dublin.

As the sunset burns over the hills in almost unbearable beauty, as the sea turns silver, and the first stars hang above the dark slopes of Croaghaun, you sigh . . . then you sigh again.

It is one of those places which a man locks up in his heart, promising himself that some day he will go back there – some day.

It was raining with a grim, quiet persistence as I left Sligo and took the road through Bundoran into Donegal.

In the wide square a few drovers stood with long sticks while a few cattle stood about and blundered on the pavement. Now and then carts laden with turf or vegetables set off through the drizzle down the road. Ireland is full of towns whose names have gone round the world with a kind of splendour to them, so that the stranger, expecting towers and turrets and great crowds, comes instead with a kind of wonder to a little town like Donegal where men huddle in the drizzle and a few calves low sadly on the pavement.

This is natural; for the fame of these places has been spread abroad by many exiles. Their greatness is founded on home-sickness.

Donegal Bay is one of the most magnificent bays in Ireland. But the beauty of this country is the glory of hill and the splendour of cliffs that fall sharply to the sea.

The rain was a mist that hid the hill-tops and hung out at sea like a white cloth. I went to the edges of cliffs and looked through the mist on waves thundering and breaking furiously against the rocks; and all round me were the formless shadows of hills: hills jutting out into the sea; hills piled back against the land; hills sage-green and smooth in the downpour.

Donegal is surely the most enchanting place in Ireland. Connemara is tribal and epic; Donegal is softer. If anything lies buried beneath the stony acres of Connemara it would be a battle-axe lost in some old fight; but in Donegal you might expect to unearth a crock of gold.

It is worthwhile to endure an Atlantic storm in these hills for the sake of that moment towards evening when it blows itself out and the rain no longer falls. The clouds thin, the blue 'Dutchman's waistcoat' shows in the watery greyness, and an unearthly beauty falls over the land. The countryside is suddenly transfigured. There is a stack of turf in a field. A moment ago it was merely a damp pyramid of peat standing on the edge of a seam. Now with this sudden magic light upon it a queer new value comes to it: it stands out importantly and holds the attention. The little trickle of peat water at the edge of the seam gains colour. The sky has flown down into it. And, lo, all round you is the same transfiguration: hills come out of the mist and stand up boldly blue as the sea; a lark takes to the sky, a plover wheels and cries above the green bogland; the little oddly-shaped stone walls shine out on the blue hills; white cabins shine; a girl with a shawl over her head comes along the road driving a donkey; and there is something in all this like a fairy-tale. You look at her, half-expecting that she will come to you and tell you that she is a princess in disguise; half-expecting that the poor moth-eaten little beast will lift an eye to you and indicate in some sure dumb way that he, poor fellow, is searching for the enchanted rose.

This light that turns Donegal into a poem for

Next page *Three Wise Kings, Straide Abbey, Co. Mayo*

151

Carrickbraghey, Co. Donegal

A horse carrying turf panniers, Clare Island

an hour, or for only a second, is a terrible and disturbing thing. If any man with a sense of beauty were compelled to see it every day it would unfit him for the practical business of life. I think that if ever Ireland produces a Joan of Arc the angel will come to her as she is driving an old grey donkey down the road in Donegal after the lifting of a storm.

My last days in Ireland were back in the East, north of Dublin. I came by mid-day into a magnificent example of a prosperous Irish market town – Dundalk.

Everything that can happen in an Irish market town was happening in Dundalk. The wide central place before the town hall was packed with people; and I have never seen so many women taking part in an Irish market day. Carts were piled up in the main street. Calves mooed under string nets. Pigs squealed and grunted. Geese hissed and gobbled. On trestles before the town hall were set out all sorts of things from silk stockings to tin buckets. Strange and alien in this typical Irish crowd was one of those Orientals who hopelessly peddle rugs and bits of bright cloth round the world. He was a young fellow and he spoke rather bad English. He told me that he was born near Calcutta:

'How do you get on in Ireland? How do they treat you? Where do you live?'

'The Irish – good peoples,' he said. 'Kind peoples. They let me sleep in stables and they give food. I know Scotland too. Good people there far north in the mountains but in the south not so good. They think you come to steal. But the Irish kind, good peoples, share food with you. Oh, very nice and very kind....'

I thought that this was rather a fine tribute from a helpless and pointless visitor to these shores.

A surprising sight in Dundalk is the Chapel of King's College, Cambridge! It is called the Pro-Cathedral of St Patrick, and it is an excellent and beautiful smaller version of King's College.

I had lunch in a room full of the biggest and the loudest Irish farmers I have ever encountered. We had tepid soup and the carelessly cooked meat served in so many Irish hotels. There is absolutely no imagination in Irish cooking. The quality of the food is perfect. Where else do you get such butter, such fresh eggs, such bacon and such meat, and such vegetables straight from a garden? One of the mysteries of Ireland is the way these things become either definitely unpleasant and even uneatable after they have passed through a kitchen! Even potatoes, which are supposed to be an Irish speciality, are often either pounded into a watery mess or are just frankly objectionable. I do not know whether there is an Irish school of cookery. I feel that Irishwomen do not enjoy cooking as Scotswomen do. Nothing pleases a Scotswoman more than if you praise her scones or her soup or her oat cakes – specially her soup, and nearly every Scotswoman can make soup that casts the best and most intricate concoctions of a French *chef* for ever into the outer darkness. But in Ireland you often forget the food because of the bright and cheerful maids who set it down before you. It was so in this place. We drank beer and passed the bread to one another and talked about the price of calves, pigs, ducks, geese and acres. It was like an Irish Salisbury. There was a robustness and a frank heartiness about this gathering of men from Louth and Meath and

Cavan quite unlike the silent, furtive gatherings in the south. All the time a buxom wench with soft blue eyes passed round, giving us food and addressing the farmers by name.

Then we all trooped into another room and ponderously chaffed a barmaid who stood behind a counter catching the chaff in mid-air and tossing it back with interest in the neatest and swiftest manner of Wimbledon. As we sat, booming away, we could hear through the open windows the mooing and cackling and barking and gabbling of Dundalk.

Then we tramped heavily out into the main street to conclude our business. I like Dundalk. I don't care how soon I go back to another of its market days.

Drogheda. . . .

This ancient town stands full of heavy memories on the estuary of the River Boyne. A great Elizabethan gate spans its streets and there are ruins like old teeth, brown and jagged, many of which go back to the bad times of Cromwell. It was here that Cromwell made clear his intention to subdue the Irish nation and stamp out its consistent demand for independence. He turned his cannon on Drogheda, battered down its walls, slew every tenth man in the garrison and sent the rest as slaves to the Barbados.

Not far from Drogheda are the famous ruins of Monasterboice. More interesting than the ruins of the round tower are the Celtic crosses. The Great Cross is nearly 1,000 years old and it stands twenty-seven feet in height, covered

Above *High Cross, Kells, Co. Meath*

Lough Cullen, Co. Mayo

Opposite page *The Aasleagh Falls, Co. Mayo*

with sculptured figures depicting Biblical scenes. One shows, or is thought to show, Christ between a band of armed men in Gethsemane. Our Lord wears the cloak of an Irish chieftain of the period, while his enemies have the long beards of Vikings. There are two other magnificent crosses, Muiredach's Cross and the Cross of Columcille. Many people have said that the faces of these crosses are exactly like those of modern Irishmen. Padraic Colum says that he can recognize likenesses of two particular friends of his!

A mile above Drogheda you come to the site of the Battle of the Boyne. When James II could not take the town of Derry he decided to risk his fortune on a pitched battle. William III had landed at Carrickfergus with a varied army of raw English recruits and hardened foreign mercenaries: French, Fins, Swedes, Danes, Dutch and Brandenburgers. Anyone who saw this army on the march must have felt that it adequately represented the international interests at stake: Protestant Europe versus the French Catholic stalking-horse, the luckless James. I have already said that the Pope was unofficially on the Protestant side, which makes it difficult to see why Catholics and Protestants can still feel sore about the Boyne!

James, with his army of 25,000 men, occupied the height of Donore Hill on the south bank; William, with a much better army of 46,000, encamped on Tullyesker Hill on the north bank. This was on the last day of June 1690. In the early morning William rode out to reconnoitre the ground and was struck on the shoulder by a cannon ball. He was not hurt, although the rumour spread that he was dead. On the next morning the battle began. William's army was split up into three divisions and advanced to ford the Boyne. The first division, the right wing, attempted the crossing at Slane; the famous Blue Guards of the Dutch army, ten abreast, entered the water opposite Oldbridge to attack the centre of the Jacobite army; William himself led his cavalry.

The Irish Dragoons put up a magnificent defence. They held the river for an hour in the face of a raking fire. They drove the infantry back into the water and met sabre charges of greatly superior strength. In this assault the great Schomberg was killed. The Williamite army eventually reached the opposite bank. They outflanked the French troops. James's French general, Lauzun, flung his infantry, his artillery and the cavalry under Patrick Sarsfield to drive back the enemy, thus leaving the centre without cannon. But there was no hope. The Irish horse made charge after charge, but bit by bit the Jacobite forces were pressed back in retreat to fall at bay late at night at Duleek. But the battle was won. James fled, taking Ireland's best soldier, Sarsfield, with him in command of the bodyguard. The losses on both sides were about a thousand killed and wounded.

'Change kings,' Sarsfield is reported to have cried before he left the battle-field, 'and we will fight you again.'

And the calm, weedy river runs on to the sea beneath a summer sky, gentle, remote from all passion, unconscious of the things that men have done upon the banks.

I came to the Hill of Tara as a man should at sunset, and alone, to say goodbye to Ireland. The sun was low in the west and soon the night mists would fall over the grasslands of Meath.

Croagh Patrick Pilgrimage

Five broad ways once led to the Hill through all the provinces; but now there is nothing but the wind in the grass and the sound of sheep. Ireland is full of old unhappy things that strangely shake the heart; and this mound of earth is one of them, lonely, remote and withdrawn like 'something left on earth after a judgment day'. The figure of St Patrick, mitred and crozier in hand, stood against the sunset. He made the sign of the Cross over Ireland. Near him an old stone leaned upward from the grass, the Lia Fail.

And as I stood there in this queerly alive place memories of Ireland came to me, little happy pictures sharp as in sunlight: the homes of Ireland, the kindness, the laughter, the music, cabins of the West white on the hill, the smell of turf fires, the light throbbing in the sky, lapwings tumbling over wild marshland, the stone walls, the green light shining on the edge of peat seams, the wild wind of the moor and all the little winding roads among the hills.

When my feet first trod Irish soil I felt that I had come to a magic country and now, as I said goodbye, I knew it truly as an enchanted island. That minor note which is like a vibration in the air, something that lives in the light and in the water and in the soil, runs through every Irish thing, but, like the cry of a bat, it is too high to be heard. But a man is conscious of it everywhere.

Some day, I thought, a great Irishman will stand upon this hill and make faith with Ireland. He will take the story of his country in strong hands and give it to the world. He will love the past of Ireland as much as he believes in her future. In him the unhappy Irish trick of looking backward instead of forward will spend itself, and Ireland, sure of her future, will forget old wounds. And this man will do for her what

Walter Scott did for Scotland: he will fuse two races and unite his country and make it whole. He will bring to Ireland the love and affection of the world. I like to think of him as a blend of north and south, a mingling of Catholic and Protestant. The southerner in him will watch the past and the northerner will reach forward into the future.

The future is with Ireland. She is the only European country, with the exception perhaps of Spain, which is not dehumanized by industrialism. The typical Irishman is the only eternal figure the world has known: the man who guides a plough. . . .

The sun sets, and the Hill grows dark. I know that in the West at this moment men are raking the ashes of the turf fires. In thousands of little white cabins they are kneeling before the wide hearth, piling up the ashes round the red glow, and in the morning there will be new light.

The shadows have fallen over the fields of Meath. The air is grey with night. St Patrick rises up over the mounds of Tara, his hand uplifted. And in the silence and darkness I listen again for that hidden music. It is not for my ears. I hear nothing but the night wind in the grass; and I say goodbye to Ireland.

ACKNOWLEDGEMENTS

For photographic permissions, acknowledgement is made to the following:
Irish Tourist Board: page 1, 6, 10, 14, 16, 18, 22, 25, 27, 29, 30, 45, 47, 50, 51, 55, 57, 58, 60, 68, 72, 75, 80, 85, 88, 95, 96, 98, 105, 111, 116, 121, 123, 124, 128, 131, 141, 142, 144, 147, 149, 154 (right), 155, 156
Tony Stone Associates: 2, 84, 100, 105, 136
J. Allan Cash: 8, 32, 36, 40, 42, 44, 49, 62, 64, 87, 89, 102, 114, 118, 143, 146, 147, 150, 151, 154 (left), 158
National Museum of Ireland: 12, 35
A. F. Kersting: endpapers, 21, 126
Peter Baker: 38, 46, 54, 56, 64, 65, 75, 76, 78, 83, 86, 90, 92, 94, 96, 106, 112, 116, 132, 134, 140, 157
Commissioners of Public Works in Ireland: 52, 57, 61, 66, 138, 139, 151
Pix Photos: 59
Eric G. Meadows: 99, 108
Colin Curwood: 159
The map was drawn by Neil Hyslop.